PROBLEMS IN EUROPEAN CIVILIZATION

THE NAZI REVOLUTION

Germany's Guilt or Germany's Fate?

EDITED AND WITH AN INTRODUCTION BY

John L. Snell, TULANE UNIVERSITY

D. C. HEATH AND COMPANY · BOSTON

In the case of sale outside the United States, special acknowledgment is made to Odhams Press Ltd. for permission to reprint the selection from Alan Bullock's HITLER: A STUDY IN TYRANNY; to Hamish Hamilton Ltd. for the selection from A. J. P. Taylor's THE COURSE OF GERMAN HISTORY; and to Routledge & Kegan Paul Ltd. for Zevedei Barbu's DEMOCRACY AND DICTATORSHIP: THEIR PSYCHOLOGY AND PATTERNS OF LIFE.

Table of Contents

Introduction

HISTORY is not an exact science. Even when it tries most to attain ultimate truth, it remains an "art of the possible." Each historian's truth about the past is in some part a personal truth; it is "subjective." The earlier the student of history acknowledges this limitation of history as a discipline the better, for indeed the greatest of all faults is to be conscious of none.

But the warning of a wise Dutch historian, J. Huizinga, is appropriate here: "A gentle slope leads from an unavoidably subjective approach to problems down to crass prejudice and partisanship." Like all knowledge, an awareness of the relativity of historical truth can be a dangerous thing. One reader might conclude that any man's interpretation of the past is as good as the next. Another student of history might decide that he should not be a student of history at all, since it will give him few absolute answers to important questions. These conclusions are not the ones this collection of historical interpretations of Nazism is designed to suggest. Scientific ideals, "myths," are as essential in the life of mankind as are "social myths." Realization that the ideal of absolutely "objective" truth cannot be achieved should lead neither to opportunism nor to despair, but to a more critical, wiser, and therefore more realistic striving to achieve it. It should lead to the study of as many different serious approaches to truth as can be found in varying historical interpretations of important events.

The readings in this booklet are extracts from varying and important interpretations of a major historical event. They are organized around a central question. The event: One of the most important developments in the history of the modern world, the creation of a twelve-year reign of terror by National Socialism under the ruthless leadership of Adolf Hitler. The central question is the question of causation: How was it possible for the Nazis to come to power in one of the most civilized countries of Europe in the twentieth century, just fourteen years after that country had thrown its monarchical armor on the slag heap of history and wrapped itself in the clothing of democratic republicanism? Did it happen because of unique conditions in Germany? Were other nations chiefly or partly responsible? These are the questions Germany's famed historian, the late Friedrich Meinecke, had in mind in 1948 when he told his German colleagues: ". . . we must rediscover ourselves by throwing light upon the historical transformations of our own character and the interweaving of our guilt and our fate." Will Nazism happen again? If so, is it likely to happen in Germany only, or might it happen elsewhere? The answers depend upon how we answer the central questions which these readings pose: *What brought Hitler to total power in Germany in 1933? Was his success and the German-European tragedy Germany's guilt or Germany's fate?*

Historians have given diverse answers to these questions. Some writers have even denied that there was a Nazi "revolution," insisting that the Nazi movement was reactionary and could have been at most a "counter-revolution." Others agree that there was a Nazi revolution but insist that it did not precede, but followed Hitler's appointment as Chancellor on January 30, 1933. Probably only the most narrowly loyal Communist historians would argue today that all that followed 1933 was counter-revolution, not revolution. It was revolutionary, let us say, in somewhat the way the rule of Cromwell was revolutionary in mid-seventeenth century England, or the way in which Napoleon was revolutionary in France after 1799. The readings in this booklet suggest both revolutionary and reactionary forces that helped prepare the way for "the Nazi Revolution" by enabling Hitler to become Chancellor of the German Reich. One of your tasks is to decide which were the more fundamental, which were immediately decisive.

Each of the units of readings presented in this booklet emphasizes the significance of a different factor in the rise of the Nazis to power. The first unit will appeal to scholars who believe that history is powerfully shaped by leading personalities in history, for it points to the importance of Hitler in the rise of Nazism. Even those like Friedrich Meinecke who emphasize other factors have acknowledged "the monstrous effect of Hitler's personality" as a cause of Nazi success. Advocates of "the great man" theory of historical causation will find much to support their convictions in the brilliant interpretation of Adolf Hitler by Alan Bullock which opens these readings.

Others look elsewhere for the causes of the Nazi revolution. "Hitler's wickedness is one thing," an English historian has written, but "how he came to be in a position to exercise his wickedness in the way he did, . . . by whose derelictions of duty, on the part not only of Germans but also of English and French and Americans and others, is another thing; and it is with the latter that, first and foremost, the historian has to do." In a spirit akin to this, Ludwig Dehio has found very impersonal reasons of a European, not a specifically German character, for the Nazi revolution. Germany was bound by some unkind historical destiny to gamble for domination — "hegemony" — in Europe, Dehio writes in the second unit in this book. Germany's gamble was only the last in a long line of similar efforts by Spain, Austria, and France to put an end to "balance of power" rivalries in Europe by imposing their own

rule. In his basic thesis, Dehio, a noted German historian, seems to make excuses for Germany. But it is well to remember that Dehio has also demanded that his fellow Germans recognize "the frightful role which we have played, as the last and therefore the most demoniacal hegemonic power of old Europe in decline."

The second essay in unit two is by a leading French historian, Maurice Baumont. He also illustrates how Germany's international political situation helped Hitler climb to power. Not some cosmic or historical destiny, but the peacemakers who wrote the Versailles Treaty of 1919 are brought to our attention by the Baumont statement. Most Germans today will still contend that the Treaty of Versailles was primarily responsible for the rise of Nazism. Certainly it provided Hitler with an excellent propaganda weapon, for it was regarded as anathema by virtually all Germans. When the terms first became known they were denounced in the German National Assembly at Weimar by all party spokesmen. The words of Ludwig Quidde, a leading German pacifist, were harsh and prophetic: "What a tragedy it would be for the human race, if these conditions should really be imposed!" Though he had many political enemies, Quidde was cheered from left to right as he shouted that Germany's motto must be: "No! And again No! — and for a third time, No!" Today, some forty years later, "Versailles" is still not forgotten in Germany. In January, 1958, Germans soberly took note of the twenty-fifth anniversary of Hitler's appointment as Chancellor. One of their most influential newspapers, the *Kölnische Rundschau* (January 30, 1958), cautioned that the failure to revise the Versailles Treaty was being repeated by the maintenance of the Yalta and Potsdam terms of 1945.

An old and typical German trick to "shake down" the West? So say those who believe that German "national character" was responsible for the Nazi revolution. Even a few German writers, and a good many German emigrants, have emphasized the role of German national character in producing the Nazi dictatorship. The German people "have always tended to worship force," writes one; "they are always impressed by the cavalryman's boot and a fist banged upon the table." Another German historian, Karl Dietrich Bracher, writes that it was, "above all," "the weaknesses of the liberal, democratic political conscience in Germany" that caused Hitler's triumph. This basic thesis is presented even more strongly by an English writer, T. L. Jarman. Concluding that the Germans "are not good material for democracy," Jarman writes that to understand why and how the Nazi regime was established "it is necessary to look back into the past of German history and to study the factors which have made the German people what they are."

Few contemporary experts on Germany insist that an allegedly innate and unchanging German "national character" made Nazism inevitable. But most experts do agree that Germany's national *characteristics* of 1932–1933 were important factors in Hitler's success, and western historians have been fond of tracing the rise of these characteristics in modern German history. Some have begun the story of Nazi authoritarianism with Martin Luther. Others, through their own types of "metahistory," have discovered the sources of Hitler's "metapolitics" in the literary romanticism of nineteenth century Germany. Still other writers treat Friedrich Nietzsche, Germany's most important philosopher of the late nineteenth century, as a forerunner of Nazism, or find antecedents of Nazism in the writings of Paul de Lagarde, Julius Langbehn, Houston Stewart Chamberlain, and Moeller van den Bruck. These are not new theories. It was a favorite technique of French propaganda in World War I to quote the words of German writers as proof of the unique character of German nationalism and ruthlessness. Nietzsche and Schopenhauer were quoted more often than Bismarck, and the historian Heinrich Treitschke, more often than Kaiser William II. By extension, several students of Nazism

have argued that a number of German intellectuals of 1918–1933 helped prepare the climate of opinion upon which Nazism throve. Few responsible scholars, if any, would suggest that the twentieth-century German writers constitute one of the three of four *major* factors that put Hitler into office. But they made their contribution.

None of the scholars who seek the causes of Nazism in German historical development have been so prolific as the noted French specialist, Edmond Vermeil. Emphasizing the cultural roots of Nazism, Vermeil wrote in 1939 that Nazism was "a simplified theology and a crude caricature [*une forme dégénérée et décadente*] of the German intellectual tradition." In his post-1945 writings he views the period 1888–1918 (the "Wilhelmian" period) as a cradle of Nazism, a period of "permanent crisis," in which the historian can easily find traits which announce the onset of "*la tragedie hitlérienne.*" In the third section, below, Vermeil sets forth his views about the pre-World War I roots of Nazism. The Vermeil reading is followed by one from a widely known book by A. J. P. Taylor, a prolific English specialist in the history of modern Germany. Taylor, like Vermeil, thinks that German history was bound to produce something like the Nazi movement. Eugene N. Anderson concludes this section by agreeing that German history failed to cultivate democratic virtues, but Anderson directly challenges the notion that "Nazism grew inevitably from the German past."

The readings that follow the Anderson statement focus upon two post-1918 German conditions, anti-Semitism and anti-Communism. The important thing to determine here is whether these were really *causes* or *results* of the rise of Nazism. Certainly they were dominant themes in Nazi propaganda. Why? Alan Bullock suggests that Hitler and other leading Nazis adopted anti-Semitic policies because they personally believed in anti-Semitism. "Hitler's anti-Semitism is the master-idea which embraces the whole span of his thought," Bullock writes. Other writers, like Vermeil, have suggested that anti-Semitism was well developed among the German people before Hitler appeared and that the Nazis adopted it because it was good politics. Some scholars have argued, to the contrary, that the often-alleged "inborn antipathy of Germans to Jews . . . may be dismissed as pure myth," while others insist that political anti-Semitism results from economic developments, rising in periods of economic crisis as economic ills are blamed upon a convenient scape-goat. But this does not explain the lack of a similarly virulent anti-Semitism in other nations in times of economic crisis. (The percentage of unemployed in the total population was about the same in the United States as in Germany in 1932.)

Several American scholars have suggested that anti-Semitism was more a result than a cause of Nazism. According to their theory, the Nazis artificially built up anti-Semitism in Germany through propaganda in a process of "polarisation," making the Jew a symbol of "evil" to match the Nazi "good" symbol, pure Aryanism. The distorted image of the Jew was made a symbol of both internal and international danger to Germany. The reading below on the role of anti-Semitism in the rise of Nazism is by Léon Poliakov of Paris, one of the world's foremost authorities on Nazi anti-Semitism, who supports the view that anti-Semitism was "essentially a means toward the general ends envisaged by National Socialism."

The Nazis capitalized upon fear of Communism as well as upon hatred of Jews in their propaganda of 1930–1933. The German Communist Party then was the largest in all of Europe outside of Soviet Russia. The German Communists, for their part, did much to earn a large measure of responsibility for Nazi success. Several scholars have shown that the German Communists placed a slavish loyalty to Moscow far above any national concern for Germany. The Communists, like the Nazis, frankly stated that they hoped to overthrow the parliamentary government of the Weimar Republic. The Communists continued un-

til 1935 to preach to German workers that not Nazism but the Social Democratic Party (S.P.D.), the most republican party in Germany, was the number one enemy of the German proletariat. Even after the Nazis seized power the Communist International advised German party members that Hitler's dictatorship would only create mass unrest and, therefore, accelerate "the speed of the development of Germany toward the proletarian revolution." Meanwhile, as the reading from Milton Mayer's book shows (page 33) many Germans had turned to Nazism to save Germany from the real and exaggerated threat of Communism.

Other writers believe that the Great Depression of the early 1930's was the most important reason for Hitler's rise to power. Still others look beyond the depression itself and blame the economic system which, they contend, produced it. Nazism flourished in a period when economic determinism was most popular in the western world as a theory of historical causation. Applied to the rise of Nazism not only by Communists but by many non-Communist scholars, it has offered one of the most widely accepted interpretations of the reasons for Hitler's success. The theory that Nazism was caused by the failure of capitalism obviously singles out a universal, not a uniquely German, reason for the Nazi revolution. The fact that Hitler's advent to power came in the midst of a great world depression lent weight to this interpretation. It has been presented in its most impressive form by the late Franz Neumann. Neumann insisted that neither the Versailles Treaty nor international Communism caused the growth of Nazism. The fifth section (see page 35) presents the essence of Neumann's complex and comprehensive interpretation of the causes of Nazi success. His basic analysis is supplemented and partly corrected by the American historian G. W. F. Hallgarten, in his discussion of the financing of Nazism by leaders of German heavy industry.

A very different set of causes of the rise of Nazism is set forth in unit six of this booklet. The first reading there is from the pen of Friedrich Meinecke, who suggests that German Socialism played an important part in building up the climate of opinion in Germany which made possible Hitler's popularity. This has not yet become a commonly accepted interpretation, chiefly because *as parties* the German Social Democratic Party (S.P.D.) was the most resolute enemy of Hitler's "National Socialist German Workers' Party" (N.S.D.A.P.). But the author of a recent book on revolutionary movements writes that: "When people are ripe for a mass movement, they are usually ripe for any effective movement, and not solely one with a particular doctrine or program."[1] And it is interesting to compare the characteristic features of the Nazi personality with the personality features which German Marxism had helped develop. The German Socialists taught millions of Germans to hate a group of fellow Germans (capitalists), much as the Nazis would later focus hatred against the Jews. Long before Hitler, the Socialists demanded strict discipline within their movement. It was they who created a vision of the world as a realm of conflict, preached the overthrow of the existing state, and fostered the notion that the German people were objects of manipulation by exploiters (for the Socialists, *German* capitalists; for the Nazis, *international* capitalists and the Versailles victor nations). The Socialists, like Nazis later, argued that the group chosen by destiny (the proletariat in Socialist theory; the German *Volk* in Nazism) could only survive by making itself the manipulator of others. For Socialists, the aim was to create a "dictatorship of the proletariat"; for Nazis, the rule of *Der Führer* in Germany and of Germany in Europe.

The Nazis advertised both Nationalism and Socialism in the official title of their party. And they unhesitatingly took over the battle vocabulary that had been used for decades by the Socialists. The noted left-Socialist, Rosa Luxemburg, *in a single page* of a single article in 1910, for example, used the following military terms that later appeared almost constantly in the Nazi vocabulary: She calls democratic reforms only small "stages" (*Etappen*) in the "march" (*Marsch*) of the proletariat to the "conquest" (*Eroberung*) of political "power" (*Macht*). She demands that the "warriors" (*Kämpfer*) against Bethmann-Hollweg, then Chancellor of Germany, become "warriors" (*Kämpfer*) for a future social order. She speaks of the alternative prospects of "victory" (*Sieg*) or "defeat" (*Niederlage*) in a "campaign" (*Kampagne*) for voting privileges, in a passionate "struggle" (*Ringen*), during which the S.P.D. should powerfully expand its *Armee* of supporters. Compare Luxemburg's sentiment and the words of the famous Socialist song, "The Internationale" ("We have been naught, we shall be all") with the following words of a Nazi song, designed to win labor support for Hitler's cause: "Sooner or later the day of revenge will come, then we will be free; working Germany, awake, break your chains asunder. We are loyally dedicated to Hitler, true unto death! Hitler will lead us out of our poverty." In 1932 the Socialists still spoke the fighting words, but from mouths that had lost their bite. The Nazis not only talked ruthlessly but acted ruthlessly. They were powerfully successful in attracting German youths who might have been rallied by a more violent Social Democracy. Less than ten per cent of the members of the S.P.D. in 1930 were under twenty-five; more members were over sixty than under twenty-five. Several million German youths, most of them from working families, reached voting age between 1928 and 1933. The Nazis won more of this youth than did any other party, though for many it was only "a toss up" whether they would "join the Communists or the Nazis."[2]

After Hitler became Chancellor, the Nazi propaganda pose as the party of the working man was continued. The leading

[1] Eric Hoffer, *The True Believer: Thoughts on the Nature of Mass Movements* (New York, 1951), 16.

[2] Hoffer, *The True Believer*, 16.

Nazi newspaper, the *Völkischer Beobachter*, on February 1, 1933, published a cartoon-drawing which symbolically showed a German laborer, collar open, rolling up his Swastika-banded shirt sleeves, going to work. Many German factories were then closed; but in the background of this drawing, factory chimneys belched forth black streamers of smoke, sooty promises of employment for all. The caption read: "To Work! The Future Is Ours." The slogan was one German Socialists had used for two generations. The Nazis expropriated Socialist slogans as part of their own ideological currency in the market for votes, just as they stole the technique of mass demonstrations and put the vivid red of Socialist banners in their own flags and drapes. True, most of the older industrial workers remained loyal to the Social Democratic Party and the Socialist trade unions. But the unions failed in 1932–1933 to take firm action to stop the rise of Nazism. That failure must surely rank as one of the most important causes of Nazi success in 1932–1933. It is discussed in the article by Gerard Braunthal which follows the Meinecke reading.

German Socialists as well as many non-Socialist historians will insist that the reasons for the Nazi revolution must be found elsewhere. They refuse to see in Nazism a culmination of Socialism, and point to the operations of reactionary forces. They insist that the leaders of German industry, that German militarism and the army leaders, or that the Prussian nobles (Junkers) were responsible for the Nazi revolution because in 1933 they made Hitler Chancellor of Germany. The argument that the Junkers caused Hitler's success appears in several of the essays in this book which concentrate upon other factors. It must receive some attention here.

The Junkers never had any use for parliamentary government. Five years before the outbreak of World War I, one of their most cantankerous deputies in the German parliament (Reichstag) told an amazed house that the King of Prussia should be able at any time to put the Reichstag out of business with "a lieutenant and ten men." In 1933 a former corporal, Adolf Hitler, was appointed Chancellor of Germany by the President of the German Republic, Marshal Paul Hindenburg, himself a Prussian Junker. Hitler, with no apparent opposition from Hindenburg, almost immediately wrecked the German Reichstag and destroyed the political parties through which representative government functioned. At this stage, many Prussian Junkers saw in a dictatorship the embodiment of a century of Junker dreams. Members of the Hohenzollern family supported Hitler, expecting him to reestablish their dynasty in a revived German monarchy. The Junkers hoped to use Hitler as a stable boy to sweep out the "mess in Berlin" and hold their bridle; the Prussian nobility, they thought, would wear the spurs, carry the whip, and ride the horse. Their hopes were soon disappointed, but the help they gave Hitler has caused many writers to blame the traditionally anti-democratic Prussian nobles for the Nazi dictatorship. The historical thesis that Junkers caused the Nazi dictatorship provided important implications for Allied social and political policy in Germany after 1945.

This thesis is closely associated with the argument that militarism and the German army were responsible for Hitler's success. Nobles occupied controlling positions in the German army, even under the Weimar Republic. In 1925 no fewer than twenty-three of the German generals on active service (forty-two) were nobles. For centuries Junkers as officers had drilled obedience into the people of Prussia, and they had affected large numbers since the beginning of universal military service in the nineteenth century. In the seventh section of this booklet, J. J. Schokking of the University of Cologne emphatically sets forth his conviction that this militarization of German thought and social processes was the indispensable development that made Nazism successful in Germany.

The First World War greatly accentuated, brutalized, and spread the spirit of militarism in Germany. Unable to readjust to civilian life, many storm-trooper veterans joined volunteer brigades as freebooters against German Communists at home and the Poles on the eastern frontier. They often wore the crooked cross, the Swastika, as an insignia. A young American historian, Robert G. L. Waite, has suggested that these products of a war-intensified militarism constituted a "Vanguard of Nazism," and he has shown that many men of the volunteer corps (*Freikorps*) of 1918–1923 subsequently became leaders of the Nazi movement. In the second reading of unit seven Waite states his thesis and catches the spirit of the *Freikorps* movement. The third selection in section seven is from the major book by an American historian, Gordon A. Craig. Craig most judiciously but firmly develops the thesis that the German generals played a decisive part in the Nazi triumph of 1933. This thesis is also set forth brilliantly and with less scholarly restraint by an English historian, John W. Wheeler-Bennett. Wheeler-Bennett portrays the supposed elevation of Hitler to power by the generals as a case study in "The Nemesis of Power." Few German scholars have agreed with this point of view.

The defense of the German generals has been presented vigorously and with distinction by Gerhard Ritter of Freiburg-im-Breisgau. A very prolific scholar and a conservative-minded member of the anti-Nazi resistance movement in World War II, Ritter has often been described since the death of Friedrich Meinecke as Germany's foremost living historian. In unit eight Gerhard Ritter succinctly discusses the role of militarism in modern Germany. He categorically states that the Nazi victory in 1932–1933 "cannot be explained by any political activity of the military."

Ritter does not stop with this defense of the honor of the old army. He has raised one of the most disturbing and important questions facing Europeans and Americans today by his insistence that it was not unique German circumstances but the operations of mass democracy that made possible the rise of such a party as the N.S.D.A.P. and the dictatorship of a demagogue such as Hitler in Germany. Ritter would agree with Wheeler-Bennett that the rise of Nazism illustrates "The Nemesis of Power." But he would insist that it was the power of the masses, not of the army, that did the harm. This belief that Nazism is a case study in the "Nemesis of democracy," not the "Nemesis of the military," finds indirect support by scholars who argue that "totalitarian democracy" has its roots "in the common stock of eighteenth-century ideas," branching out from the French Revolution. This is an old idea. It was advanced in the nineteenth century by Alexis de Tocqueville and other critics of mass democracy. Its application to the study of Nazism is relatively new, and western democratic historians have been very reluctant to recognize any kind of democracy in Nazism. But this only avoids the real problem. The all-important question here is not whether Nazism was a form of democracy but whether it was produced by democracy. Parliamentary government certainly functioned poorly in Germany in the period 1930–1933, just as it did in France and in various other states which possessed many political parties. Thus the Ritter thesis cannot be treated lightly. Before Germany's industrialists contributed much money to the Nazi party, before the Junkers decided to use Hitler as their tool, and before German generals agreed to see the corporal in the Reich Chancellory, the N.S.D.A.P. had won 37.4 percent of all the votes in free, democratic elections in July, 1932. In the same elections another 14.6 per cent of the German voters cast their ballots for another type of dictatorship by voting Communist. Thus 52 percent of the votes of July, 1932, were cast against the liberal, parliamentary regime, strong evidence for the argument that the Weimar Republic destroyed itself through the mechanism of its own highly democratic parliamentary process.

Ritter's view has been embraced in part in a recent book on modern Germany by the knowledgeable American historian Koppel S. Pinson, who rejects the previously prevalent notion that Nazism was just a movement of the lower middle class (*Kleinbürgertum;* petty bourgeoisie). He contends that the Nazi dictatorship rested upon "the following and support of millions of people who represented a true cross section of the German population." Hitler himself boasted in April, 1933, that in some parts of the Reich "up to 95 percent" of his supporters in the climb to power were peasants, and asserted that they had "perhaps the greatest part" in making possible the Nazi revolution (*Völkischer Beobachter,* April 6, 1933). Sigmund Neumann, a German-American political scientist, has especially emphasized the success of Nazism in attracting the war and postwar generations of youths of all classes in Germany. "They were material for any political revolution," Neumann writes. "Everything depended upon which generation would take up the challenge. The Nazi Revolution of 1933 decided it." Nazism, Pinson concludes, was "a product of the mass democratic society of the twentieth century," a movement that could never have succeeded without modern developments which gave the masses political influence. The statements of Ritter and Pinson suggest that the "common man" is as easily and as emotionally swayed as Hitler believed him to be. Are all three right about the common man in Germany? In Germany only? Milton Mayer returned from a year of field study after World War II convinced that it was not "German man" but "Man" who brought Nazism to power. "He happened to be in Germany under certain conditions. He might be here, under certain conditions." Could Nazism happen here? Could it happen, under another name, in France?

It depends more upon psychic conditions than upon the form of government, say the social psychologists. Nazism was a "salvationist" creed, promising hope to the hopeless, like Communism. One writer asserts that it is the fate of all salvationist creeds "to be born out of the noblest impulses of man, and to degenerate into weapons of tyranny." But social psychologists seek the causes of the tyranny not so much in the creeds as in the hopeless state of mind of the recipients. One of the most interesting efforts of this sort is a recent study by Norman Cohn. Any of several developments may cause people to be receptive to salvationist creeds and half-mad (paranoic) leaders, Cohn writes. Cohn believes that the forces that produced chiliastic movements in the Middle Ages also helped make the Nazi movement. What kind of forces does he see? Were they present in the Germany of 1918–1933? Cohn writes: "It may be that the society as a whole is deprived of its status or independence and forced into a humiliating subjection. [Versailles?] It may be that traditional offices of authority cease to fulfil their customary function and thereby forfeit prestige. . . . [The defaults of the German parliament, 1930–1933?] Or it may be that the supreme authority is discredited or disappears. [The overthrow of the monarchy in 1918?]" Cohn suggestively concludes that "calamities caused by unseen or unknown agencies — plague or famine, gross inflation or mass unemployment" may produce "an emotional disturbance so widespread and acute" that "the only way in which it can find effective relief is through an outburst of paranoia, a sudden, collective and fanatical pursuit of the Millennium."[3]

Psychic conditions similar to these were present in the Germany of 1930–1933. Is it, then, the social-psychologist, not the historian, who must tell us why the Nazi revolution occurred? A prominent American psychologist of German origins, Erich Fromm, developed his own thesis in this matter while Hitler still ruled his "Third Reich." Fromm's thesis is that individuals in the contemporary world need to feel a part of something bigger than themselves, need to feel not only freedom, but what has

[3] Norman Cohn, *The Pursuit of the Millennium* (London, 1957), 313–314.

recently been called "togetherness." Fromm put forth the thesis that the masses of Central Europe, freed from established political controls and social-psychic taboos in 1918, sought what he called an "escape from freedom." Many found the desired "belongingness" in the staged solidarity, the closed ranks of Nazi mass demonstrations. In the last section in this booklet, another social-psychologist, Zevedei Barbu, develops the thesis that Nazism was a manifestation of social pathology, that people of all classes in Germany turned to Nazism out of an aggravated collective sense of insecurity such as that which Cohn describes. An American anthropologist, the late Robert H. Lowie, closes the readings in this volume with a word of caution against generalizations about the psychology or "national character" of the German people.

Having read this booklet, you should be able to form your own tentative interpretation of the causes of the Nazi revolution.

Was it the fault of one man, Adolf Hitler? Of leading Entente statesmen, makers of the Versailles Treaty? Of the men of German industry or the German army? Of the democratic system? The theories lead from the sins of one man to fundamental philosophical and theological questions about the nature of Man in general. In forming your own explanation, you must first decide which factors were relatively most important in causing the Nazi victory. Since one interpretation is *not* just as good as any other, your own synthesis of the factors of greatest importance demands that you evaluate the qualifications and reliability of each author whose works appear here. In going beyond these extracts you might begin by reading the full books or articles from which these readings have been taken. You will find additional materials for reading or research listed in the "Suggestions for Additional Reading" at the end of this volume.

The Conflict of Opinion

". . . the foundation of Hitler's success was his own energy and ability as a political leader."

— ALAN BULLOCK

"The condition of international affairs, exploited to the limit by National-Socialism, explains to a great extent the success of Hitler. . . ."

— MAURICE BAUMONT

". . . the 'Third Reich' rested solely on German force and German impulse; it owed nothing to alien forces."

— A. J. P. TAYLOR

"Of my ten friends, only two . . . wanted to be Nazis and nothing else. They were positive — still are — that National Socialism was Germany's and therefore their own, salvation from Communism. . . ."

— MILTON MAYER

". . . the central problem was the imperialism of German monopoly capital, becoming ever more urgent with the continued growth of the process of monopolization."

— FRANZ NEUMANN

". . . the big idea that was floating in the air — the idea of the amalgamation of the nationalist and socialist movements — unquestionably found in [Hitler] the most ardent spokesman and the most determined practitioner. . . . With this idea he bribed a wide circle of citizens."

— FRIEDRICH MEINECKE

"Schleicher's chancellorship . . . was long enough for Schleicher and the generals who supported him to execute a remarkable volte-face. In early December they were determined that Hitler must not come to power. . . . By late January they were determined that he *must* come to power. . . . At this crucial moment in German history, the army command had swung to his side."

— GORDON A. CRAIG

"The rapid rise to power of the National-Socialist Party after 1931 cannot be explained by any political activity of the military." "Lacking any kind of critical ability, the masses saw in Hitler a savior and a prophet. . . ."

— GERHARD RITTER

"Why could not Socialism or Communism play this role . . . ? The answer . . . is, in essence, simple. The Nazis offered to the people the quickest and the most radical way of relief from a situation of stress and insecurity. . . . Insecurity can be considered as the main cause of German society's failure to adjust itself to twentieth-century democratic civilization. . . ."

— ZEVEDEI BARBU

HITLER MADE THE MOVEMENT

It is impossible to study the Nazi movement without acknowledging the tremendous importance of the part Adolf Hitler played in its growth and in the shaping of its character. Experts disagree about the degree of importance to attach to Hitler's personality in relation to less personal factors; but all agree that this personality was significant. Hitler's unique personal qualities—strengths and weaknesses—are brilliantly set forth in the reading below. This reading is taken from a full-length biography of Adolf Hitler, the best yet published. The author, Alan Bullock, is a noted English expert on contemporary Germany and professor of modern history at Oxford University. Many specialists in German history in Europe and America consider this biography of Hitler to be the most satisfactory over-all account yet written of the rise and fall of the Nazi movement.

The Talents of Tyranny

ALAN BULLOCK

THE FOUNDATION of Hitler's success was his own energy and ability as a political leader. Without this, the help would never have been forthcoming, or would have produced insignificant results. Hitler's genius as a politician lay in his unequalled grasp of what could be done by propaganda, and his flair for seeing how to do it. He had to learn in a hard school, on his feet night after night, arguing his case in every kind of hall, from the smoke-filled back room of a beer-cellar to the huge auditorium of the *Zirkus Krone*; often, in the early days, in the face of opposition, indifference or amused contempt; learning to hold his audience's attention, to win them over; most important of all, learning to read the minds of his audiences, finding the sensitive spots on which to hammer. "He could play like a virtuoso on the well-tempered piano of lower middleclass hearts," says Dr. Schacht. Behind that virtuosity lay years of experience as an agitator and mob orator. Hitler came to know Germany and the German people at first hand as few of Germany's other leaders ever had. By the time he came to power in 1933 there were few towns of any size in the Reich where he had not spoken. Here was one great advantage Hitler had over nearly all the politicians with whom he had to deal, his immense practical experience of politics, not in the Chancellery or the Reichstag, but in the street, the level at which elections are won, the level at which any politician must be effective if he is to carry a mass vote with him.

Hitler was the greatest demagogue in history. Those who add "only a demagogue" fail to appreciate the nature of political power in an age of mass politics. As he himself said: "To be a leader, means to be able to move masses."

From Alan Bullock, *Hitler: A Study in Tyranny* (New York, 1952), pp. 61–64, 342–348, and 352–353. Reprinted by permission of Harper and Brothers. *This and other readings in this book appear without the footnotes which are found in the original publications.*

The lessons which Hitler drew from the activities of the Austrian Social Democrats and Lueger's Christian Socialists were now tried out in Munich. Success was far from being automatic. Hitler made mistakes and had much to learn before he could persuade people to take him seriously, even on the small stage of Bavarian politics. By 1923 he was still only a provincial politician, who had not yet made any impact on national politics, and the end of 1923 saw the collapse of his movement in a fiasco. But Hitler learned from his mistakes, and by the time he came to write *Mein Kampf* in the middle of the 1920s he was able to set down quite clearly what he was trying to do, and what were the conditions of success. The pages in *Mein Kampf* in which he discusses the technique of mass propaganda and political leadership stand out in brilliant contrast with the turgid attempts to explain his entirely unoriginal political ideas.

The first and most important principle for political action laid down by Hitler is: Go to the masses. "The movement must avoid everything which may lessen or weaken its power of influencing the masses . . . because of the simple fact that no great idea, no matter how sublime or exalted, can be realized in practice without the effective power which resides in the popular masses."

Since the masses have only a poor acquaintance with abstract ideas, their reactions lie more in the domain of the feelings, where the roots of their positive as well as their negative attitudes are implanted. . . . The emotional grounds of their attitude furnish the reason for their extraordinary stability. It is always more difficult to fight against faith than against knowledge. And the driving force which has brought about the most tremendous revolutions on this earth has never been a body of scientific teaching which has gained power over the masses, but always a devotion which has inspired them, and often a kind of hysteria which has urged them into action. Whoever wishes to win over the masses must know the key that will open the door to their hearts. It is not objectivity, which is a feckless attitude, but a determined will, backed up by power where necessary.

Hitler is quite open in explaining how this is to be achieved. "The receptive powers of the masses are very restricted, and their understanding is feeble. On the other hand, they quickly forget. Such being the case, all effective propaganda must be confined to a few bare necessities and then must be expressed in a few stereotyped formulas." Hitler had nothing but scorn for the intellectuals who are always looking for something new. "Only constant repetition will finally succeed in imprinting an idea on the memory of a crowd." For the same reason it is better to stick to a programme even when certain points in it become out of date: "As soon as one point is removed from the sphere of dogmatic certainty, the discussion will not simply result in a new and better formulation, but may easily lead to endless debates and general confusion."

When you lie, tell big lies. This is what the Jews do, working on the principle, "which is quite true in itself, that in the big lie there is always a certain force of credibility; because the broad masses of a nation are always more easily corrupted in the deeper strata of their emotional nature than consciously or voluntarily, and thus in the primitive simplicity of their minds they more readily fall victims to the big lie than the small lie, since they themselves often tell small lies in little matters, but would be ashamed to resort to large-scale falsehoods. It would never come into their heads to fabricate colossal untruths and they would not believe that others could have the impudence to distort the truth so infamously. . . . The grossly impudent lie always leaves traces behind it, even after it has been nailed down."

Above all, never hesitate, never qualify what you say, never concede an inch to the other side, paint all your contrasts in black and white. This is the "very first condition which has to be fulfilled in every kind of propaganda: a systematically one-sided attitude towards every problem that has to be dealt with. . . . When they see an uncompromising onslaught against an adversary, the people have at all times taken this as proof that right is on the side of the active aggressor; but if the aggressor should go only halfway and fail to push home his success . . . the people will look upon this as a sign that he is uncertain of the justice of his own cause."

Vehemence, passion, fanaticism, these are "the great magnetic forces which alone attract the great masses; for these masses always respond to the compelling force which emanates from absolute faith in the ideas put forward, combined with an indomitable zest to fight for and defend them. . . . The doom of a nation can be averted only by a storm of glowing passion; but only those who are passionate themselves can arouse passion in others."

Hitler showed a marked preference for the spoken over the written word. "The force which ever set in motion the great historical avalanches of religious and political movements is the magic power of the spoken word. The broad masses of a population are more amenable to the appeal of rhetoric than to any other force." The employment of verbal violence, the repetition of such words as "smash," "force," "ruthless," "hatred," was deliberate. Hitler's gestures and the emotional character of his speaking, lashing himself up to a pitch of near-hysteria in which he would scream and spit out his resentment, had the same effect on an audience. Many descriptions have been given of the way in which he succeeded in communicating passion to his listeners, so that men groaned or hissed and women sobbed involuntarily, if only to relieve the tension, caught up in the spell of powerful emotions of hatred and exaltation, from which all restraint had been removed.

It was to be years yet before Hitler was able to achieve this effect on the scale of the Berlin *Sportpalast* audiences of the 1930s, but he had already begun to develop extraordinary gifts as a speaker. It was in Munich that he learned to address mass audiences of several thousands. In *Mein Kampf* he remarks that the orator's relationship with his audience is the secret of his art. "He will always follow the lead of the great mass in such a way that from the living emotion of his hearers the apt word which he needs will be suggested to him and in its turn this will go straight to the hearts of his hearers." A little later he speaks of the difficulty of overcoming emotional resistance: this cannot be done by argument, but only by an appeal to the "hidden forces" in an audience, an appeal that the orator alone can make. . . .

The extravagant conversations recorded by Hermann Rauschning for the period 1932–1934, and by Dr. Henry Picker at the Fuehrer's H.Q. for the period 1941–1942, reveal Hitler in another favourite role, that of visionary and prophet. As the French Ambassador, André François-Poncet, noted, there was in Hitler much of King Ludwig II of Bavaria. The fabulous dreams of a vast empire embracing all Europe and half Asia; the geopolitical fantasies of intercontinental wars and alliances; the plans for breeding an *élite*, biologically preselected, and founding a new Order to guard the Holy Grail of pure blood; the designs for reducing whole nations to slavery — all these are the fruits of a crude, disordered, but fertile imagination soaked in the German romanticism of the late nineteenth century, a caricature of Wagner, Nietzsche, and Schopenhauer. This was the mood in which Hitler indulged, talking far into the night, in his house on the Obersalzberg, surrounded by the remote peaks and silent forests of the Bavarian Alps; or in the Eyrie he had built six thousand feet up on the Kehlstein, above the Berghof, approached only by a mountain road blasted through the rock and a lift guarded by doors of bronze. It was also the mood in which he and Himmler drew up the blueprints and issued the orders for the construction of that New Order which was to replace the disintegrating liberal bourgeois world of the nineteenth century. After the outbreak of the war and the conquest of the greater part of Europe, all practical restraint upon Hitler's translation of his fantasies into brutal reality was removed. The S.S. extermination squads, the *Einsatzkommandos,* with their gas-vans and death camps; the planned elimination of the Jewish race; the treatment of the Poles and Russians, the Slav *Untermenschen* — these, too, were the fruits of Hitler's imagination.

All this combines to create a picture of which the best description is Hitler's own famous sentence: "I go the way that Providence dictates with the assurance of a sleepwalker." The former French Ambassador speaks of him as "a man possessed"; Hermann Rauschning writes: "Dostoevsky might well have invented him, with the morbid derangement and the pseudo-creativeness of his hysteria"; one of the Defence Counsel at the Nuremberg Trials, Dr. Dix, quoted a passage from Goethe's *Dichtung und Wahrheit* describing the Demoniac and applied this very aptly to Hitler. With Hitler, indeed, one is uncomfortably aware of never being far from the realm of the irrational.

But this is only half the truth about Hitler, for the baffling problem about this strange figure is to determine the degree to which he was swept along by a genuine belief in his own inspiration and the degree to which he deliberately exploited the irrational side of human nature, both in himself and others, with a shrewd calculation. For it is salutary to recall, before accepting the Hitler-Myth at anything like its face value, that it was Hitler who invented the myth, assiduously cultivating and manipulating it for his own ends. So long as he did this he was brilliantly successful; it was when he began to believe in his own magic, and accept the myth of himself as true, that his flair faltered.

So much has been made of the charismatic nature of Hitler's leadership that it is easy to forget the astute and cynical politician in him. It is this mixture of calcula-tion and fanaticism, with the difficulty of telling where one ends and the other begins, which is the peculiar characteristic of Hitler's personality: to ignore or underestimate either element is to present a distorted picture.

II

The link between the different sides of Hitler's character was his extraordinary capacity for self-dramatization. "This so-called *Wahnsystem,* or capacity for self-delusion," Sir Nevile Henderson, the British Ambassador, wrote, "was a regular part of his technique. It helped him both to work up his own passions and to make his people believe anything that he might think good for them." Again and again one is struck by the way in which, having once decided rationally on a course of action, Hitler would whip himself into a passion which enabled him to bear down all opposition, and provided him with the motive power to enforce his will on others. The most obvious instance of this is the synthetic fury, which he could assume or discard at will, over the treatment of German minorities abroad. When it was a question of refusing to listen to the bitter complaints of the Germans in the South Tyrol, or of uprooting the German inhabitants of the Baltic States, he sacrificed them to the needs of his Italian and Russian alliances with indifference. So long as good relations with Poland were necessary to his foreign policy he showed little interest in Poland's German minority. But when it suited his purpose to make the "intolerable wrongs" of the Austrian Nazis, or the Germans in Czechoslovakia and Poland, a ground for action against these states, he worked himself into a frenzy of indignation, with the immediate — and calculated — result that London and Paris, in their anxiety for peace, exerted increased pressure on Prague or Warsaw to show restraint and make further concessions to the German demands.

One of Hitler's most habitual devices was to place himself on the defensive, to accuse those who opposed or obstructed him of aggression and malice, and to pass rapidly from a tone of outraged innocence to the full thunders of moral indignation. It was always the other side who were to blame, and in turn he denounced the Communists, the Jews, the Republican Government, or the Czechs, the Poles, and the Bolsheviks for their "intolerable" behaviour which forced him to take drastic action in self-defense.

Hitler in a rage appeared to lose all control of himself. His face became mottled and swollen with fury, he screamed at the top of his voice, spitting out a stream of abuse, waving his arms wildly and drumming on the table or the wall with his fists. As suddenly as he had begun he would stop, smooth down his hair, straighten his collar and resume a more normal voice.

This skilful and deliberate exploitation of his own temperament extended to other moods than anger. When he wanted to persuade or win someone over he could display great charm. Until the last days of his life he retained an uncanny gift of personal magnetism which defies analysis, but which many who met him have described. This was connected with the curious power of his eyes, which are persistently said to have had some sort of hypnotic quality. Similarly, when he wanted to frighten or shock, he showed himself a master of brutal and threatening language, as in the celebrated interviews with Schuschnigg and President Hacha.

Yet another variation in his roles was the impression of concentrated will-power and intelligence, the leader in complete command of the situation and with a knowledge of the facts which dazzled the generals or ministers summoned to receive his orders. To sustain this part he drew on his remarkable memory, which enabled him to reel off complicated orders of battle, technical specifications and long lists of names and dates without a moment's hesitation. Hitler cultivated this gift of memory assiduously. The fact that subsequently the details and figures which he cited were often found to contain inaccuracies did not matter: it was the immediate effect at which he aimed. The swiftness of the transition from one mood to another was startling: one moment his eyes would be filled with tears and pleading, the next blazing with fury, or glazed with the faraway look of the visionary.

Hitler, in fact, was a consummate actor, with the actor's and orator's facility for absorbing himself in a role and convincing himself of the truth of what he was saying at the time he said it. In his early years he was often awkward and unconvincing, but with practice the part became second nature to him, and with the immense prestige of success behind him, and the resources of a powerful state at his command, there were few who could resist the impression of the piercing eyes, the Napoleonic pose and the "historic" personality.

Hitler had the gift of all great politicians for grasping the possibilities of a situation more swiftly than his opponents. He saw, as no other politician did, how to play on the grievances and resentments of the German people, as later he was to play on French and British fear of war and fear of Communism. His insistence upon preserving the forms of legality in the struggle for power showed a brilliant understanding of the way to disarm opposition, just as the way in which he undermined the independence of the German Army showed his grasp of the weaknesses of the German Officer Corps.

A German word, *Fingerspitzgefühl* — "finger-tip feeling" — which was often applied to Hitler, well describes his sense of opportunity and timing.

No matter what you attempt [Hitler told Rauschning on one occasion], if an idea is not yet mature you will not be able to realize it. Then there is only one thing to do: have patience, wait, try again, wait again. In the subconscious, the work goes on. It matures, sometimes it dies. Unless I have the inner, incorruptible conviction: *this is the solution*, I do nothing. Not even if the whole Party tries to drive me into action.

Hitler knew how to wait in 1932, when his insistence on holding out until he could secure the Chancellorship appeared to court disaster. Foreign policy provides another instance. In 1939 he showed great patience while waiting for the situation to develop after direct negotiations with Poland had broken down and while the Western Powers were seeking to reach a settlement with Soviet Russia. Clear enough about his objectives, he contrived to keep his plans flexible. The date he fixed for the invasion of Czechoslovakia, 1 October 1938, is one of the few instances in which Hitler committed himself to a definite time-table, out of fury at the way the Czechs had scored off him on 28 May. Much more characteristic was his action in the case of the annexation of Austria and the occupation of Prague, where he made the final decision on the spur of the moment.

Until he was convinced that the right moment had come Hitler would find a hundred excuses for procrastination. His hesitation in such cases was notorious: his refusal to make up his mind to stand as a Presidential candidate in 1932, and his attempt to defer taking action against Roehm and the S.A. in 1934, are two obvious examples. Once he had made up his mind to move, however, he would act boldly, taking considerable risks, as in the reoccupation of the Rhineland in 1936, or the invasion of Norway and Denmark just before the major campaign in the west.

Surprise was a favourite gambit of Hitler's, in politics, diplomacy and war: he gauged the psychological effect of sudden, unexpected hammer-blows in paralysing opposition. An illustration of his appreciation of the value of surprise and quick decision, even when on the defensive, is the second presidential campaign of 1932. It had taken Goebbels weeks to persuade Hitler to stand for the Presidency at all. The defeat in the first ballot brought Goebbels to despair; but Hitler, now that he had committed himself, with great presence of mind dictated the announcement that he would stand a second time and got it on to the streets almost before the country had learned of his defeat. In war the psychological effect of the *blitzkrieg* was just as important in Hitler's eyes as the strategic: it gave the impression that the German military machine was more than life-size, that it possessed some virtue of invincibility against which ordinary men could not defend themselves.

No régime in history has ever paid such careful attention to psychological factors in politics. Hitler was a master of mass emotion. To attend one of his big meetings was to go through an emotional experience, not to listen to an argument or a programme. Yet nothing was left to chance on these occasions. Every device for heightening the emotional intensity, every trick of the theatre was used. The Nuremberg rallies held every year in September were masterpieces of theatrical art, with the most carefully devised effects. "I had spent six years in St. Petersburg before the war in the best days of the old Russian ballet," wrote Sir Nevile Henderson, "but for grandiose beauty I have never seen a ballet to compare with it." To see the films of the Nuremberg rallies even today is to be recaptured by the hypnotic effect of thousands of men marching in perfect order, the music of the massed bands, the forest of standards and flags, the vast perspectives of the stadium, the smoking torches, the dome of searchlights. The sense of power, of force and unity was irresistible, and all converged with a mounting crescendo of excitement on the supreme moment when the Fuehrer himself made his entry. Paradoxically, the man who was most affected by such spectacles was their originator, Hitler himself, and, as Rosenberg remarks in his memoirs, they played an indispensable part in the process of self-intoxication. Hitler had grasped as no one before him what could be done with a combination of propaganda and terrorism. For the complement to the attractive power of the great spectacles was the compulsive power of the Gestapo, the S.S., and the concentration camp, heightened once again by skilful propaganda. Hitler was helped in this not only by his own perception of the sources of power in a modern urbanized mass-society, but also by possession of the technical means to manipulate them. This was a point well made by Albert Speer, Hitler's highly intelligent Minister for Armaments and War Production, in the final speech he made at his trial after the war.

Hitler's dictatorship [Speer told the court] differed in one fundamental point from all its predecessors in history. His was the first dictatorship in the present period of modern technical development, a dictatorship which made complete use of all technical means for the domination of its own country.

Through technical devices like the radio and the loud-speaker, eighty million people were deprived of independent thought. It was thereby possible to subject them to the will of one man. . . .

Earlier dictators needed highly qualified assistants, even at the lowest level, men who could think and act independently. The totalitarian system in the period of modern technical development can dispense with them; the means of communication alone make it possible to mechanize the lower leadership. As a result of this there arises the new type of the uncritical recipient of orders. . . . Another result was the far-reaching supervision of the citizens of the State and the maintenance of a high degree of secrecy for criminal acts.

The nightmare of many a man that one day nations could be dominated by technical means was all but realized in Hitler's totalitarian system.

In making use of the formidable power which was thus placed in his hands Hitler had one supreme, and fortunately rare, advantage: he had neither scruples nor inhibitions. He was a man without roots, with neither home nor family; a man who admitted no loyalties, was bound by no traditions, and felt respect neither for God nor man. Throughout his career Hitler showed

himself prepared to seize any advantage that was to be gained by lying, cunning, treachery, and unscrupulousness. He demanded the sacrifice of millions of German lives for the sacred cause of Germany, but in the last year of the war was ready to destroy Germany rather than surrender his power or admit defeat.

Wary and secretive, he entertained a universal distrust. He admitted no one to his counsels. He never let down his guard, or gave himself away. This is reflected in the almost total absence of any correspondence apart from official letters such as those he wrote to Mussolini. Hitler rarely committed himself to paper. "He never," Schacht wrote, "let slip an unconsidered word. He never said what he did not intend to say and he never blurted out a secret. Everything was the result of cold calculation." . . .

Cynical though he was, Hitler's cynicism stopped short of his own person: he came to believe that he was a man with a mission, marked out by Providence, and therefore exempt from the ordinary canons of human conduct.

Hitler probably held some such belief about himself from an early period. It was clear enough in the speech he made at his trial in 1924, and after he came out of prison those near him noticed that he began to hold aloof, to set a barrier between himself and his followers. After he came to power it became more noticeable. It was in March, 1936, that he made the famous assertion already quoted: 'I go the way that Providence dictates with the assurance of a sleep-walker.' In 1937 he told an audience at Würzburg:

However weak the individual may be when compared with the omnipotence and will of Providence, yet at the moment when he acts as Providence would have him act he becomes immeasurably strong. Then there streams down upon him that force which has marked all greatness in the world's history. And when I look back only on the five years which lie behind us, then I feel that I am justified in saying: That has not been the work of man alone.

Just before the occupation of Austria, in February, 1938, he declared in the Reichstag:

Above all, a man who feels it his duty at such an hour to assume the leadership of his people is not responsible to the laws of parliamentary usage or to a particular democratic conception, but solely to the mission placed upon him. And anyone who interferes with this mission is an enemy of the people.

It was in this sense of mission that Hitler, a man who believed neither in God nor in conscience ("a Jewish invention, a blemish like circumcision"), found both justification and absolution. He was the Siegfried come to reawaken Germany to greatness, for whom morality, suffering and "the litany of private virtues" were irrelevant. It was by such dreams that he sustained the ruthlessness and determination of his will. So long as this sense of mission was balanced by the cynical calculations of the politician, it represented a source of strength,

but success was fatal. When half Europe lay at his feet and all need of restraint was removed, Hitler abandoned himself entirely to megalomania. He became convinced of his own infallibility. But when he began to look to the image he had created to work miracles of its own accord — instead of exploiting it — his gifts deteriorated and his intuition deluded him. Ironically, failure sprang from the same capacity which brought him success, his power of self-dramatization, his ability to convince himself. His belief in his power to work miracles kept him going when the more sceptical Mussolini faltered. Hitler played out his "world-historical" role to the bitter end. But it was this same belief which curtained him in illusion and blinded him to what was actually happening, leading him into that arrogant overestimate of his own genius which brought him to defeat. The sin which Hitler committed was that which the ancient Greeks called *hybris*, the sin of overweening pride, of believing himself to be more than a man. If ever a man was destroyed by the image he had created it was Adolf Hitler. . . .

A PRODUCT OF EUROPEAN
POWER POLITICS

International politics and specifically the Versailles Treaty of 1919 are often cited as causes of the success of Nazism in Germany. In the first reading presented in this section, Ludwig Dehio argues that the First World War and the harsh treaty of 1919 changed German national character, preparing it for Nazism. The author is saying, in brief, that the causes and the nature of Nazism are rooted in the old national state structure of Europe, with its "balance of power" politics and recurrent efforts by one state or another to establish its preponderance, its hegemony. Dehio rejects, therefore, Vermeil's argument that pre-1914 German thought and national characteristics laid the foundation for the growth of Nazism. The important article from which Dehio's argument is taken appeared first in 1952 in Germany's outstanding historical journal, the *Historische Zeitschrift*, which Dehio edited from its postwar revival in 1949 until 1956.

 In the second reading in this section a noted French historian, Maurice Baumont, shows more specifically how Hitler made use of German grievances against the treaty settlement of 1919 in his early efforts to climb to power. Baumont is the author of several important books and one of the world's foremost experts on European international relations between 1918 and 1939.

Germany and the Epoch of World Wars

LUDWIG DEHIO

A FTER YEARS of political passivity, Germany is now coming back into a position of self-responsibility. More than ever she now needs to understand clearly the period of the two world wars — the period that preceded her exclusion from self-responsibility. In discussing this problem here, we can only state our views with aphoristic brevity. We shall merely mark a number of points which, linked together, may indicate a rough profile of events.

First, let us state our guiding idea. It is adapted, I think, to serving as the central point in this discussion, or indeed in any discussion that strives to rise to a third position above current accusations and defences — to a historical picture standing by its own strength. I have in mind the idea of struggle for hegemony. For, each of the two world wars, like two consecutive acts in the same tragedy, displays in the most exacerbated form possible the familiar gen-

From Hans Kohn (ed.), *German History: Some New German Views* (Boston, 1954), pp. 122–125, 128–130. Reprinted by permission of the Beacon Press, Inc.

eric traits of those great European wars associated with the names of Charles V and Philip II, Louis XIV and Napoleon I.

I shall make no effort to support this thesis by comparison and analysis of everything which happened in the whole broad field of relations between the great powers of Europe. But I will try to make use of such comparative analysis in considering the history of Germany, especially in our period and in domestic policy. Here we may profitably use another idea — the idea of the demoniac character (*Dämonie*) of power. It is not difficult to show its close connexion with our initial conception. It impressed itself very strongly upon our minds mainly during the Second World War, the most recent struggle for European hegemony. By attaching preponderant importance to my central idea, I am compelled to reject other explanations at least in part. This is particularly true of those interpretations which view German history in our period as a thing apart, like a tree rising straight from roots in German soil. They fail to keep in mind how tangled the history of Germany is with that of other lands. . . . If you take my position, that Germany was *the* hegemonic power of our time, then you avoid both errors. For on the one hand, Germany, in her very function as a hegemonic power, presents herself to us with characteristics utterly unlike those of her fellow-members in the family of nations. But on the other hand, it seems certain to us that Germany did not always have her own distinct personality! Consideration of events from a broader historical view warns us to pass judgment cautiously. When we look back over the history of the old hegemonic powers we do gain caution, for then we become aware that many of the characteristics of modern Germany which, when we see them only in terms of the twentieth century, impress us as being uniquely German, were anticipated by the earlier hegemonic powers, to say the very least. Thus, when these modern German characteristics are considered in terms of the earlier centuries, they appear typical. Of

course, this comparative investigation of the past makes us aware of the precise degree of unique significance within the whole series of hegemonic wars which should be attached to the two such wars fought by Germany. In the last analysis, when we make comparisons with past or contemporary phenomena, as the case may be, this is the conclusion which emerges with ever greater distinctness and certainty.

The victim of the demoniac character of power, however, is flung about in a turbulent storm by overpowering will-to-rule and amoral joy of battle. Inevitably, such demoniac character bursts out vigorously in that most comprehensive and violent of all struggles on earth, the struggle for hegemony. Then, since the hegemonic power towers above these struggles in lonely preeminence, before it are placed demonic temptations of a specific kind. . . .

German history was chiefly continental until the turn of this century. It then suddenly entered the arena of supreme and worldwide decisions, in which no matter how great the struggle upon the Continent, events on the sea are more important than even the most spectacular land battles. We wish now to pose a question: How was the First World War, not caused, but made possible? This is our answer. As a world war, beyond question it was made possible by the vigorous efforts of rejuvenated Germany to expand. As yet, such efforts on the part of Russia alone could not then have brought it about. It took on, none the less, the classic form of a struggle for European hegemony because of England's reaction.

. . . In the conflict with a world of enemies filled with hatred and slander we experienced an intensification of our character which in 1914 brought us a feeling of bliss. But in this sudden spiritual isolation brought about by our political isolation, there was already present the seed of over-intensification of our character. This development, foreseen only by a clear-headed few, was rapidly brought closer by the foolhardy passions of the many. Over-intensification shattered the psychic balance of the nation. Hemmed in by hatred, it responded with hatred. Then for the first time came the spread of extremist and monomanic ideas which, under the conditions of a quieter development, would probably only have been able to maintain themselves on the fringes of society.

The most clear-sighted, consulting the oracle of our domestic reason of state, endeavoured with great vigour to break out of this vicious circle. But the obscure replies of the oracle could only increase the confusion. The Seven Years War had not been a hegemonic war. The strategy of attrition on land lost meaning when our adversary, by his attrition policy on the sea, began to win the upper hand. Despite a noble moderation, those who called for amicable negotiation of a peace settlement were unable to estimate exactly the capacities of the insular foe. Meanwhile, sinister ideas made their way among us like the words of Max Weber, "Let them hate, as long as they fear," or the threat by Otto Hintze, "At the very worst, we will let ourselves be buried beneath the ruins of European civilization."

Such things pointed to the future. On the whole, however, we may say that the development of the demoniacal character of German hegemonic aspirations reached only the first stage during the First World War. It did not as yet wreck the structure of existing society and morality, or of the historic state and its traditions, although it was already undermining that structure. In any case, the forces of civilization were eroding the foundations of the structure. These demoniacal forces were still loyal, unrevolutionary; to that degree, they called to mind the struggle of the Spanish and French monarchs, rather than those of the French Revolution and Napoleon.

That changed completely in the first years of peace, when the demoniac character of German hegemonic aspirations became more evident. How could such an unanticipated development occur? In our discussion of this problem we will consider both what happened to Germany and what happened in Germany.

The termination of earlier hegemonic wars established peace for generations. This had still been successfully achieved in 1815 when a peace was made which at one and the same time imposed its terms on the vanquished and won them by reconciliation. But how could the victor of 1919 actually establish such an enduring peace according to the old prescriptions? The very foundation of the old system of peace treaties, the European system, was gravely damaged. On the one hand, Russia was not only forced out of it but was also transformed into a graver danger than ever for the West. On the other hand, America was drawn in, after Europe for the first time had proved unable by its own efforts to bring the hegemonic threat under control. How was it possible, in so confused a situation, to create something durable? It was probably possible only in the Western area. Even then it could never be achieved without America, the militarily decisive power in the West. Likewise, it required a new creative idea, which Wilson brought over. What he proposed was not renewal of the European system with its hegemonic wars, not establishment of a world system with corresponding dangers, but rather total abolition of foreign policy in the old sense as such, that is, total abolition of a plurality of sovereign states, each ready to wage war. Hence, he proposed peaceful unification of the peoples into a global commonwealth under Anglo-Saxon leadership. What a marvelous change in the world he heralded! Or was it destined to remain in the realm of wonderful fantasies? Until then the insular system, represented by England, had traditionally opposed the newly risen power on the Continent. The insular system was now represented by America, a new power, which held ideas which appeared to most European statesmen at the time to be arrogantly simple minded, but which seemed like an evangel to the masses. To the Germans these ideas stood for release from the narrow limitations of their situation, to be brought about by the peaceful disarmament of the old system, with its stranglehold. It therefore appeared to be a miraculous solution of the German problem.

But the danger to the shattered psychic balance of our nation was all the greater, for the miracle remained a dream. On the heels of the catastrophe of war came the disaster of peace. Old Europe thereby won out over the newcomer, America. The outworn European system was put into operation again. The wave on which men rode did not carry them forward, but backwards. This was one of the most important explanations of the evils to come. . . .

The Role of Foreign Policy in the Success of the National Socialist Party

MAURICE BAUMONT

THE TREATIES of Versailles and Saint-Germain, the reparations, and the occupation of the Ruhr, provided excellent material for a nationalism which condemned the humiliations and the injustice of which Germany was regarded as the victim. The condition of international affairs, exploited to the limit by National Socialism, explains to a great extent the success of Hitler, the demagogue, who, as the mouthpiece of a Germany determined to avenge her defeat, claimed to lead the fight for the liberation of the German people.

The embryo of Hitlerism is an inexorable nationalism, and by what might be called an historical law of proportion, the advances of National-Socialism follow upon a general surge of nationalism. Indeed, many of the elements of Hitlerism existed before Hitler, particularly the Pangermanist and ultra-nationalist aspirations of which his propaganda made the utmost use. It is not necessary to examine here this problem, which always arises, as soon as one considers the causes of the rapid growth of National-Socialism. . . .

We are not concerned here with a discussion of the very serious faults of the Treaty of Versailles. We shall merely indicate that these faults, immeasurably exaggerated by strong feeling, raised such criticism, not only in Germany but in almost every country, that international opinion generally sided violently against the treaty which had rapidly become unpopular. This semi-Wilsonian treaty, which was neither a peace of total victory nor of moderate compromise, was furiously attacked by its principal English and Italian authors, and as early as 1920 it was disowned by the Americans. Born mainly of American inspiration, it was henceforward vitiated at its very source. It was rejected by the United States, and Russia had not been present at Versailles. It was branded in "the neutral countries" as the principal cause of growing economic and political difficulties. Under the title "The Slandered Peace" — rightly or wrongly — Etienne Mantoux showed that the Treaty of Versailles was not as badly drawn up, or as disastrous in its "economic consequences" as had been maintained by Keynes, the

From Maurice Baumont, John H. E. Fried, Edmond Vermeil, and others, *The Third Reich* (New York, 1955), pp. 456, 472–473, and 475–477. Reprinted by permission of Frederick A. Praeger, Inc.

famous British economist; it had become the butt of general criticism which was hindering its execution. It came to be generally believed that Germany could not live under the Treaty of Versailles.

Instinctively and in a frenzy of national passion, Germany confronted the irreducible differences of the Allies with her opposition to a hard treaty, in which she claimed to see a systematic programme of pillage for the benefit of inhuman masters, ingeniously concealed under a pretext of moral guilt.

Criticism of the Treaty of Versailles provided an admirable element of agitation, from which Hitler resolved to draw the maximum advantage. All the arguments tirelessly and methodically used to build a case against the great injustice of Versailles were used and amplified in Hitler's speeches. He had not invented them; he only took them up again with passionate violence, and repeated them unceasingly. Tirelessly he would return to the same topics. As early as 1923, in Munich, General von Lossow observed that "Hitler's long speeches contained almost always the same things." Hitler raged against "the infamous treaties of Versailles and Saint-Germain," and in a general way against what he called the treaties signed "in the suburbs of Paris." For he was not one to allow "German children to be deprived of their daily bread for love of peace." . . .

The Weimar diplomacy was invariably accused of complying with all Allied demands. Hitler scourged its "contemptible cowardice." He was determined to bring to a halt the policy of boundless compliance by "a Germany ready to accept anything imposed upon her." He condemned the "criminal," "senseless," "catastrophic" policy, which abandoned national interests, and the "cringing servility" to foreign countries. "Irresponsibility and incompetence" had until then guided German policy.

Hitler mercilessly attacked the German pacifists: the "foolishness of incorrigible dreamers." The German pacifist would be "silent about the most outrageous violence committed against the nation. . . . He does not think of vengeance or even of defence." Every time the people were threatened he would consider on which side objective justice lay. This "cursed objectivity" poisoned the heart, and the "lulling chatter of the whining cowards" would have to come to an end.

It was time to recover outward independence in a spirit of decisiveness and purpose. An independent, vigorous, and dynamic German state would have to come into being again.

Every instance of "foreign pressure" on Germany gave Hitler the opportunity to increase his prestige as agitator. The furious exaltation of patriotic exuberance discredited the rulers, accused of stupid and criminal weakness. Hitler recalled Clausewitz with the words, "an honour stained by cowardly submission can never be wiped clean." He derided the Weimar Government's patient efforts methodically to take advantage of the lengthy prevarications over disarmament, as it had been conceived at Versailles, the victors having to submit to the same disarmament obligations as the vanquished and being bound to follow Germany's example later. . . .

Like the German nationalists, the National-Socialists refused to follow Stresemann's supple diplomacy, which, according to Count Westarp, went "from illusion to deception, and from deception to a new illusion." In a spirit of defiance they would not agree that Germany should proclaim herself averse to regaining "German lands" by force. They would not accept the surrender of Alsace-Lorraine. The National-Socialists accused Stresemann of leading Germany from one disaster to another by his policy of negotiation.

After suffering a serious setback in the 1928 elections, which only gave him twelve seats in parliament, Hitler began to act the part of a political personality, and not only a propaganda mouthpiece. For, early in 1929, he contracted an alliance with Hugenberg in order to wage a campaign against the Young Plan, which was to re place the Dawes Plan. A violent campaign was started against the "tribute" imposed on Germany by the Young Plan, which would "condemn the German people to slavery for the remainder of the twentieth century." At the end of 1929 a plebiscite was held "against the Young Plan and against the lie of the war debts." This great idea of Hugenberg allowed Hitler to use to his own advantage the formidable propaganda instrument which that press and film magnate controlled. Hugenberg's machine gave the National-Socialist orators a wide hearing.

The plebiscite collected only four million votes during the first round, and 5,600,000 during the second — figures below those polled by the right wing in the 1928 election. The serious and genuinely active elements of the right-wing opposition seemed at that time to be formed not by the brown militia of Nazism, but by the impressive association of the *Stahlhelm*.

When Hindenburg signed the Young Plan on 13th March 1930, Rosenberg declared that "Hindenburg having taken leave of Germany, Germany equally takes leave of him." Strasser called for "the heads of those who signed the Young Plan." . . .

In order to block the advance of a growing National-Socialism, those in power attempted to wrest from it its nationalist propaganda arguments. Their efforts to bring reparations to a halt succeeded; they were practically stopped. After the Hoover moratorium (20th June 1931), the Lausanne agreement, on which Papen prided himself, was concluded on 9th July 1932. The burden of reparations was almost entirely abolished.

Once the question of reparations was settled, German foreign policy made great forward strides towards equal rights in the matter of armaments. This equality of rights, demanded in the form of the reconstitution of a large German army, was discussed in principle on 11th December 1932 at the disarmament conference, France being prepared to follow the lead of the United States, Great Britain, and Italy in this matter.

Already considerations of foreign policy had ceased to be serious factors in the advance of National-Socialism. The masses no longer thought of the Versailles Treaty, now that foreign soldiers no longer trod on German soil, and the burden of reparations had come to an end.

The eyes of the masses were now fixed upon home affairs, and "work and bread" took the first place in their demands. In this respect, there is no doubt that Hitler's decisive success had its source in the economic and social crisis of 1930–1932, with its disastrous unemployment. It was not on an issue of foreign policy that the number of National-Socialist votes rose from 2.6 per cent in 1928 to 18.3 per cent in 1930. At any rate it was not the determining factor. . . .

AN OUTGROWTH OF GERMAN HISTORY?

Edmond Vermeil, professor of history at the Sorbonne, has been for some years the most widely known French interpreter of modern German history. He finds the causes of Nazism not in the policies of non-Germans, but in the unique development of modern Germany, especially in German intellectual developments in the nineteenth century. Though distasteful to most German historians, Vermeil's approach to an understanding of Nazism has been very popular in the English-speaking world. The first reading in this section is taken from a one-volume English language abridgment of Vermeil's two-volume work, *L'Allemagne Contemporaine*. In the second reading a prominent Oxford University historian, A. J .P. Taylor, further develops the thesis that Nazism was a logical—even inevitable—outgrowth of German historical development. This belief in the uniqueness of German history is challenged in the third reading by Eugene N. Anderson, author of several studies in the history of Germany and professor of history at the University of California at Los Angeles.

Pre-1914 Roots

EDMOND VERMEIL

BISMARCKIAN Germany was divided between two great Christian faiths, the Evangelical Lutheran bloc of North Germany opposing the Catholic regions of Bavaria, Rhenish Prussia, Westphalia, and Poland. Between these two were five regions of mixed faith — Hesse, the Palatinate, Baden, Württemberg, and Silesia. In 1890 there were altogether 31 million Lutheran or reformed Protestants in the Reich, and some 18 million Catholics. While the Protestants were spread among various groups or political parties, the Catholics by contrast were gathered into a single party — the Centre (Zentrum), which defended the interests of their faith. Indeed, the Centre was in a better position to protect its interests than the twenty-eight Protestant churches, which were territorial in character.

Lutheranism directed the political, social, and cultural history of Germany into attitudes of mind and conceptions of collective life which were handed down from generation to generation. A Germany that had remained Catholic or become converted to Calvinism would have had very different destinies; she would have been more distinctly Western, for Lutheran religious ideas, which embraced forms of territorialism, generally caused Germans in the various regions to abandon political thought and action for what they called *Obrigkeit*, a sort of monarchism with an authoritarian bent founded upon a mixture of civil and religious power.

From Edmond Vermeil, *Germany in the Twentieth Century* (New York, 1956), pp. 14–20 and 31. Reprinted by permission of Frederick A. Praeger, Inc.

If, in addition to the influence of territorial Lutheranism, we take into account the influences of Counter-Reformation Catholicism and Romantic idealism, from which the twentieth-century national ideology stems, we can understand the German social *mystique*. To Germans this meant the organic State, the new Reich conceived as a planned community, more or less solidly established upon the compromises which Bismarck tried to integrate within his Empire — Prussia and the Reich, unitary and federal institutions, monarchy and Parliament, agriculture and industry, Lutheranism and Catholicism, capitalism and socialism. Here was the *Volkstum*, the popular totality of Germany.

Henceforth, because of this *rapprochement* between political thought and the religious spirit, national might came to be treated as an end in itself, justifying every means. It was the true source of imperialism, of power politics, of that singular Machiavellism which seems to reveal itself at every instance in German history. It is the proper meaning of the term "political realism." Collective Machiavellism offered the Germans three prospects. The first was political indifference, an escape from the harsh authority of the State to find refuge in inward piety or in Utopianism, just as classical cosmopolitanism had once done. The second offered itself when the Wars of the [French] Revolution and of the Empire revealed to Germany her own impotence, and led her no further to separate the private sphere from the State sphere, but individual morality from political Machiavellism. . . .

Why, then, should there be anti-Semitism in a country where the Christian faiths played so important a part of public life? We have noted how Germany had always been a State with a leader at its head, but not a society led by a true élite. For this reason Germany, unlike England and France, did not possess a social element with powers of leadership that could integrate the Jews settled in the country within the national life. Jewry therefore remained an alien body, despite its immense influence. The tragedy of the German Jews came about because they lived like those ill-assorted couples between whom there is perpetual tension owing to a lack of strength and firmness in the two parties. Here, perhaps, lies the most probable explanation of that anti-Semitism which was later to be the *leitmotiv* of the Hitlerites. Its solid roots, its most profound origins, however, lay in the Bismarckian Empire.

German Jews were emancipated by the law of 1869. They looked upon the new Reich as a kind of *terra nova,* as another New World to conquer, where they would be sure of economic, social, and cultural advantages superior to those in the East, and even in the West. They quickly gained prominence in industrial circles, stimulated political and economic liberalism, and at the same time took an interest in the aspirations of the proletariat. They were, moreover, needed in the world of science, of the Press, of literature and art, and in important matters touching international affairs.

However, their situation changed after the financial crisis of 1873, in which they were involved. They were chosen to play the scapegoat so as to absolve the Gentiles from responsibility for the disaster. Pamphlets stressed the antithesis between *German* and *Jew,* accusing the Jew of wishing to dominate the German world and of fostering both large-scale capitalism and Marxism in it.

If the chief aim of the Imperial Government was to win the confidence of the working class, to turn it away from international Marxism, and so consolidate the social position of the middle classes, who were seeking shelter with the State and the industrialist employers, then the measures adopted by the middle classes between 1919 and 1935 may be said to have originated during the reign of William II. The Churches directed their claims and their hopes. They did not yet know that there would be anti-Christianity as well as anti-Semitism one day.

From 1881 so-called "Social Christianity"

broke loose against the Jews. Pastor Stöcker, chaplain to the Imperial Court, led the offensive. Bismarck resisted and curbed the anti-Semitic movement, because, realist that he was, he respected the superiority of the Jews in business. No doubt it later became apparent that the social agitation of Pastor Stöcker could be as dangerous as that of the Social Democrats. The young Emperor dropped him very quickly, but anti-Semitism, defending a monarchy of divine right and the middle class, had received its impetus, and was soon to penetrate the countryside and the small towns. Under William and during the twentieth century it was not slow to combine with racialism. While the two Christian faiths tended to become united as the foreign situation grew more complex, the idea of a "Germanic" Christianity, as formulated by H. S. Chamberlain in his famous *Foundations of the Nineteenth Century*, took hold of people's minds. It was favoured by Pan-Germanism and encouraged by the Emperor.

CULTURE IN PERIL

The problem of the relationship between militarism and culture engaged the attention of numerous writers during the time of William II. They asked themselves whether the Germany of Bismarck, dedicated to the rule of bureaucracy, industry, and arms, was destined to create a true civilization, to unite the myrtle and the sword. The question assumed full significance only if the term militarism were given a wide meaning. It was applicable not only to activities directly connected with the Army, but also to professional work involving discipline, conscientious labour, constant intensity of energy, and that rigidity of thought and attitude which, in the German, nearly always verges upon the pedantic.

Nietzsche showed why the German State, with its unwieldy armour, its thousands of bureaucrats, engineers, and technicians, ran a strong risk of destroying all higher culture in Germany, and of breaking with the true spiritual traditions of the nation. It was just this radical pessimism

that the Pan-Germanists opposed with their crude optimism. They took up again the theme of Latin and Western decadence, vying with each other in celebrating German virtues and affirming that Germany could remain strong by creating the most refined civilization, or, if they preferred, could create it by remaining strong. From 1890 the *Rembrandt Deutsche* of Julius Langbehn proclaimed the union of Christianity and militarism, while in his *Foundations of the Nineteenth Century* H. S. Chamberlain claimed that the Germans alone were capable of purifying the religion and culture of Europe. On the eve of war a certain Friedrich Lange saw in Prussian militarism the purest emanation of culture in Germany. Such theories, and their success among the cultivated élite and the average public, were evidence of the dangers threatening humanism in Wilhelmian Germany. Modern instruction and new teaching methods with a bias towards technical realism, the triumph of irrationalism in philosophy, the crisis in literature, and other symptoms in their turn bore witness to a certain intellectual and moral unbalance, which was not to escape analysis by the historian.

In his youthful writings, and right up to his final works, Nietzsche put German culture as he saw it on the morrow of the Franco-German War on trial. Naturally he adopted a highly superior point of view, casting a saddened eye upon the gymnasiums and the modern schools. In the former classical culture was rapidly degenerating, and, though technical instruction has its legitimate demands, it was none the less true that, more than anywhere else, in Germany instruction and culture were confused. Both science and art suffered from this decline; journalistic style destroyed the taste for a style of expression which conformed to the great traditions of the past. Nobody saw more clearly than Nietzsche the tragic breach which, in the Bismarckian Empire, was opening between ancient classicism and the new tendencies in education.

During the Wilhelmian era German philosophy seemed to be moving in three directions. Some, while sacrificing everything to Nietzsche's relativism, strove none the less to justify objective science. Others, extending Nietzschean irrationalism beyond its natural limits, explored the unconscious basis of the human being — those forces and instincts that Nietzsche himself had christened "Dionysian." Finally, it was at this time that the early outlines of existentialism were drawn. . . .

Nietzsche had established a clear distinction between the Dionysiac unconscious and the intellect, between a kind of initial barbarism, the sign of powerful vitality, and evolved thinking, the product of refined civilizations. And he wondered if, in contrast to the force of the elementary instincts, there was not a secret threat of degeneracy in societies which had grown old and become separated from their original vitalism.

This irrationalism, which was soon to end in the racialism of the Pan-Germanists and of the Hitlerites, played a determining part in the German thought of this period. Both in the individual and in society it was the manifestation of obscure forces that tended to destroy the refuges provided by thought and by religion to protect human weakness. From Jean-Jacques Rousseau to Schelling, then to Eduard von Hartmann, a tradition was formed which placed unconscious life in the foreground of inquiry. Here Freudianism had its point of departure, and here, too, arose the danger of extreme irrationalism, from which Richard Wagner was not exempt, and which, shortly after 1871, was to pass from Karl Bachofen to the Nietzsche of *Die Geburt der Tragödie*.

Later, in a study of Germany's moral and intellectual situation, Karl Jaspers spoke of the seductive appeal launched by those pretending to substitute the sombre, mysterious realities of the unconscious, of the blood, of mystical faith, of the soil and of the terrestrial Dionysian instinct for the clarities of the consciousness. Such views were found again under the Third Reich in Hitlerite doctrine and in the "German Faith Movement." On the one hand were the philosophers, who restored rationalism and scientific objectivity to their rightful places; on the other hand was the irrationalism, visionary and nocturnal, of the pseudo-philosophers, the belief that unconscious life was of greater interest than the clear, conscious activities of its ends.

The link between educative and philosophical conceptions and literature is easily seen. While humanism and science had to defend themselves against both industrial mechanization and excessive taste for the mysteries of the unconscious life, there was a division among the writers — between the novelists and dramatists, who dealt with social problems, and the poets, who raised up the inner shrine.

Thus Wilhelmian Germany oscillated between a fierce, implacable industrial rationalization and this mystical communion which was its counterpart. When war broke out in 1914 precious few thinkers, writers, or artists in Germany could resist the delirium of collective enthusiasm and the freeing of national ambitions. They found themselves defenceless before this inruption (*Durchbruch*) of Germanism in Europe, before the barbarism which had long been simmering under the thin crust of Wilhelmian culture. . . .

In the cultural sense also certain currents bore the nation in similar directions. Mechanized industry and science with a predilection for biology encouraged a mentality which had already been created by the communal *mystique* of Romanticism. Moreover, it must be admitted that the Nietzschean ideology of the Will to Power furnished the future Nazis with parts of their doctrine once it had been misinterpreted and distorted, and once its real meaning had been twisted. The Pan-Germanism of the Kaiser's day, when it had been vulgarized and padded out with anti-Semitism, directly inspired National Socialism. . . .

History Unfolds, 1918-1933

A. J. P. TAYLOR

THE REPUBLIC created by the Constituent Assembly at Weimar lasted in theory for fourteen years, from 1919 to 1933. Its real life was shorter. Its first four years were consumed in the political and economic confusion which followed the Four Years' War; in its last three years there was a temporary dictatorship, half cloaked in legality, which reduced the republic to a sham long before it was openly overthrown. Only for six years did Germany lead a life ostensibly democratic, ostensibly pacific; but in the eyes of many foreign observers these six years appeared as the normal, the "true" Germany, from which the preceding centuries and the subsequent decade of German history were an aberration. A deeper investigation might have found for these six years other causes than the beauty of the German character. . . .

The appointment of Brüning as Chancellor in March 1930 marked the end of the German republic. Germany had slipped back without effort to the days just before defeat when, too, a Roman Catholic Chancellor had carried out the orders of Hindenburg. Then it had been the ultimatum from Supreme Headquarters, now it was the "emergency decree," by which Germany was ruled; both were signed by the same hand. The "crisis" of March 1930, which brought Brüning into power, was the deliberate manufacture of the army leaders, and especially of General Schleicher, the army specialist for political intrigue. The decline in world trade, the increase in unemployment, had hardly begun; the only crisis was that even in the years of prosperity the budget had failed to balance. The "national" classes still drew the line at direct taxation; and it was to impose direct taxes that Müller, Social Democratic Chancellor of a coalition government, proposed to use emergency decrees. But Schleicher and his associates would not put Hindenburg's prestige behind a democratic government; for while the Social Democrats did not impede German rearmament they would not actively promote it. On the other hand, the "national" party leaders were too wild: if called to office, they would at once denounce the Young Plan and overthrow the shell of the constitution. The Reichswehr leaders were not driven on by a demagogic demand: quite the reverse, their action provoked the demagogic demand. When Brüning became Chancellor there were only twelve National Socialists in the Reichstag; it was owing to his policy that in the general election of September 1930, 108 National Socialists were returned. The National Socialist victory, abhorrent to Brüning, unwelcome to the Reichswehr, was the inevitable outcome of Brüning's dictatorship.

The "crisis" of March 1930 was provoked by the Reichswehr, and Brüning chosen as Chancellor, for the sole purpose of speeding up German rearmament. The economic crisis was an after-thought, an accident, which took the Reichswehr by surprise. The Reichswehr leaders stood behind Brüning, gave him assurance against disorder, enabled him to disregard, as Imperial Chancellors had done, defeat in the Reichstag. Brüning, in return, pushed on rearmament, redoubled the campaign against the remnants of Versailles, yet,

From A. J. P. Taylor, *The Course of German History: A Survey of the Development of Germany since 1815* (New York, 1946), pp. 189–192 and 203–214. Reprinted by permission of Coward-McCann, Inc.

being a member of the Centre, served as window-dressing both to Germans of the Left and to the Allies, who, forgetting his activities during the Four Years' War, failed to see in the pious Roman Catholic the spokesman of German militarism. Yet Brüning's position was sincere enough: wishing to serve Germany, he could serve only the army. Moreover in promoting rearmament he was pursuing a policy in which he himself believed: thus being in a superior position to all other Centre politicians, whether under the Empire or of the republic, who were indifferent to the policies which they executed. The army was the sole "authority": that was the key to Brüning's position. The republic had failed to develop a "governing class." The middle classes, themselves in awe of authority, had never forgiven the republic for the defeat of 1918; the working classes, with no social revolution to inspire them, were loyal, devoted, but ineffective. The economic crisis of 1929–33 did not give the deathblow to the republic; at most it drew attention to the fact that the republic was dead. Any system can stand in fair weather; it is tested when the storm begins to blow. This test the German republic could not pass: with few supporters and no roots, it fell at the first rumble of thunder.

In 1930 parliamentary rule ceased in Germany. There followed, first, temporary dictatorship, then permanent dictatorship. Technically the Reichstag remained sovereign (as it does to the present day); actually Germany was ruled by emergency decrees, which the democratic parties tolerated as the "lesser evil" — the greater evil being to provoke a civil conflict in defence of democracy. Unemployment, the result of the economic crisis, sapped the spirit of the skilled workers, who were the only reliable republicans. Their skill had been the one secure possession to survive the inflation; unemployment made it as worthless as the paper savings of the middle classes. Therefore, though still loyal to the republic, they became half-hearted, indifferent to events, feeling that they stood for a cause

which was already lost, ready to respond, though with shame, to a "national" appeal. The depression, too, completed the demoralization of the respectable middle class. The brief period of prosperity had stimulated a tendency, or its beginning, to postpone "revenge" to a distant future — just as French pacifism after 1871 began as a very temporary affair. Of course Versailles had to be destroyed, but not while profits were mounting, not while salaries were good, not while more and more bureaucratic posts were being created; the German bourgeoisie felt that their generation had done enough for Germany. But in 1930, with the ending of prosperity, the distant future of "revenge" arrived: the crisis seemed almost a punishment for the wickedness of neglecting the restoration of German honour and power. As for the great capitalists, they welcomed the depression, for it enabled them to carry still further the process of rationalization, which had been its cause. As one of them exclaimed: "This is the crisis we need!" They could shake off both the remnants of Allied control and the weak ineffective brake of the republic, could make their monopolies still bigger, could compel even the Allies to welcome German rearmament as the only alternative to social revolution.

The republic had been an empty shell; still its open supersession in 1930 created a revolutionary atmosphere, in which projects of universal upheaval could flourish. Now, if ever, was the time of the Communists, who saw their prophecies of capitalist collapse come true. But the Communists made nothing of their opportunity; they still regarded the Social Democrats as their chief enemy, still strove to increase confusion and disorder in the belief that a revolutionary situation would carry them automatically into power. The German Communists, with their pseudorevolutionary jargon, were silly enough to evolve this theory themselves; but they were prompted on their way by the orders of the Comintern, which was still obsessed with the fear of a capitalist intervention against the

Soviet Union and so desired above everything else to break the democratic link between Germany and western Europe. The Soviet leaders, with their old-fashioned Marxist outlook, thought that the German army leaders were still drawn exclusively from the Prussian Junkers and therefore counted confidently on a renewal of the old Russo-Prussian friendship. In 1930 German democracy was probably too far gone to have been saved by any change of policy; still the Communist line prevented the united front of Communist and Social Democratic workers which was the last hope of the republic. The Communists were not very effective; so far as they had an effect at all it was to add to the political demoralization, to act as the pioneers for violence and dishonesty, to prepare the way for a party which had in very truth freed itself from the shackles of "bourgeois morality," even from the morality devised by the German bourgeois thinker, Karl Marx.

To talk of a "party," however, is to echo the misunderstandings of those lamentable years. The National Socialists were not a party in any political sense, but a movement: they were action without thought, the union of all those who had lost their bearings and asked only a change of circumstances no matter what. At the heart of the National Socialists were the Free Corps, the wild mercenaries of the post-war years, whose "patriotism" had taken the form of shooting German workers. The Munich rising in November 1923 had been the last splutter of their Free Corps days. Since then they had been taught discipline by a ruthless gangster leader, Hitler, a man bent on destruction, "the unknown soldier of the last war," but unfortunately not buried, expressing in every turn of his personality the bitter disillusionment of the trenches; and a greater master of hysteric oratory than either Frederick William IV or William II. The National Socialists had no programme, still less a defined class interest; they stood simply for destruction and action, not contradictory but complementary. They united in their ranks the

disillusioned of every class: the army officer who had failed to find a place in civil life; the ruined capitalist; the unemployed worker; but, most of all, the "white collar" worker of the lower middle class, on whom the greatest burden of the post-war years had fallen. The unemployed clerk; the university student who had failed in his examinations; the incompetent lawyer and the blundering doctor: all these could exchange their shabby threadbare suits for the smart uniforms of the National Socialist army and could find in Hitler's promise of action new hope for themselves. In England they would have been shipped off to the colonies as remittance men: their presence in Germany was the high price which the victors of 1918 paid for the worthless tracts of German colonial territory.

The failure of the Munich rising in 1923 had taught Hitler a bitter lesson: he must not run head on against the army and the possessing classes. From that moment until September 1933 he used the method of intrigue, of terror and persuasion, not the method of open assault. Just as the Communists had tried to outbid the "national" parties in whipping up nationalist passion, so now Hitler outbid the Communists, but with the added attraction, for the upper classes, that this nationalist passion would be turned against the German working classes as well. He was at once everyone's enemy and everyone's friend: his programme of contradictory principles could succeed only in a community which had already lost all unity and self-confidence. To the workers he offered employment; to the lower middle classes a new self-respect and importance; to the capitalists vaster profits and freedom from trade union restraints; to the army leaders a great army; to all Germans German supremacy; to all the world peace. In reality it mattered little what he offered: to a Germany still bewildered by defeat he offered action, success, undefined achievement, all the sensations of a revolution without the pains. In September 1930, when the economic crisis had hardly begun, but when the French had evacuated the Rhineland, the National Socialists were already hot on the heels of the Social Democrats as the largest party in the Reichstag; the "national" card was irresistible.

This moral was drawn too by Brüning, who, in his hatred of National Socialist paganism, adopted in succession almost every item of the National Socialist creed. Called in to save German capitalism and to promote German rearmament, Brüning went further on the path already marked out by Stresemann. Stresemann had tried to make the republic popular by winning concessions in foreign affairs. Brüning demanded concessions in foreign affairs in order to win support for his system of presidential dictatorship. If Germany was allowed to rearm, the Germans might not notice the reductions in their wages. More than that, if Germans were brought together in a campaign of hatred against Poland, the disparities between rich and poor would be overlooked. Where Stresemann had tried to conciliate the Allies, Brüning blackmailed them: if they did not make concessions to him, they would have to deal with Hitler and the National Socialists. Brüning knew that the economic crisis was due to deflation, the decline of prices and wages; still, far from attempting to arrest or even alleviate this deflation, he drove it on — forced wages and, less effectively, prices, still lower — perhaps to get the crisis over all the sooner, perhaps to threaten the Allies with the prospect of German ruin. For the Brüning Cabinet was primarily a cabinet of "front-line fighters," officers of the Four Years' War, who were dominated by the resolve to reverse the verdict of 1918. Stresemann too had desired to liquidate Versailles, but he had cared also for democracy; Brüning was for the undoing of Versailles pure and simple, hoping, no doubt, to win popularity with the German people, satisfying still more his own deepest feelings. For him, as much as for the great capitalists, the crisis was welcome, the crisis he needed. His most ambitious effort was the customs union with

Austria in March 1931, ostensibly a measure against the depression, though it is difficult to see the use of a customs union between two countries both suffering from unemployment and impoverishment. In reality the purpose of the customs union was not economic, but demagogic, an evocation of the programme of Greater Germany, and, so far as it had any sense, a move of economic war against Czechoslovakia, exposed outpost of the system of Versailles. France and her central European allies protested and, almost for the last time, got their way: the separation of Austria from Germany was the only remaining guarantee against an overwhelming German power, and this last fragment of victory was shored up for a few more years.

The Brüning policy of combating evil by taking homeopathic doses of the same medicine, far from checking the National Socialists, aided their advance. If the Allies trembled before Brüning's blackmail, they would collapse altogether before the blackmail of Hitler. Brüning made everyone in Germany talk once more of rearmament, of union with Austria, of the injustice of the eastern frontier; and every sentence of their talk made them turn, not to Brüning, but to the movement of radical revision. Above all, Brüning had overlooked the lesson of the Four Years' War which Ludendorff had learnt too late — that a programme of German power must rest on a demagogic basis. Austria, Poland, Bohemia, could not be conquered, and Versailles defied, by a Chancellor supported only by a section of the Centre party; for that, a united German will was needed. Captain Brüning was half-way between General Ludendorff and Corporal Hitler, with the weaknesses of both, the advantages of neither. Brüning, the defender of the Roman Catholic Church, shared the error of Stresemann, the defender of the republic: both thought to draw the sting of nationalism by going with it, to silence demagogy by trying to capture its tone. Neither grasped that his every step strengthened his enemy; neither understood that the only security for German democracy, or for German Christian civilization, lay in a full and sincere acceptance of the Treaty of Versailles. Only if Germany made reparation; only if Germany remained disarmed; only if the German frontiers were final; only, above all, if the Germans accepted the Slav peoples as their equals, was there any chance of a stable, peaceful, civilized Germany. No man did more than Brüning to make this Germany impossible.

The decay, disappearance indeed, of peaceful Germany was openly revealed in 1932 when the time came to elect a new President. The candidate of upheaval and violence was Hitler; the candidate of the peaceful constitutional Left was Hindenburg, hero of the Four Years' War and candidate in 1925 of the "national" parties. The "left" had moved immeasurably to the "right" in the last seven years: what was then a defeat would now rank as a dazzling victory — for it could not be supposed that a senile soldier of over eighty and never mentally flexible had changed his outlook since 1925, or for that matter since 1918. The German people had accepted militarism: the only dispute was between the orderly militarism of a field-marshal and the unrestrained militarism of a hysterical corporal. Hindenburg carried the day, evidence that the Germans still craved to reconcile decency and power, militarism and the rule of law. Yet Hindenburg's victory, strangely enough, was the prelude to National Socialist success. Brüning drew from the presidential election the moral that his government must win greater popularity by some demagogic stroke; and, as a stroke in foreign policy was delayed, he sought for achievement in home affairs. His solution was his undoing. He planned to satisfy Social Democratic workers and Roman Catholic peasants by an attack on the great estates of eastern Germany, breaking them up for the benefit of ex-service men; and as a first step he began to investigate the affairs of the *Osthilfe*, the

scheme of agrarian relief inaugurated in 1927 by which tens of millions of pounds had been lavished on the Junker landowners. This was a programme of social revolution, and it could be carried out only with the backing of enthusiastic and united democratic parties. But Brüning's solution of Germany's ills was the restoration of the monarchy, and he would not condescend to democracy by a single gesture; he relied solely on Hindenburg, and this reliance was his undoing. For Hindenburg, once himself the patron of land settlement for ex-servicemen, had been long won over by the Junker landowners, who in 1927 had launched a plan for presenting Hindenburg with an estate at Neudeck, once a Hindenburg property, but long alienated. It was characteristic of the Junkers that even for their own cause they would not pay: all the estate owners of eastern Germany only subscribed 60,000 marks, the rest of the required million was provided by the capitalists of the Ruhr — principally by Duisberg, manufacturer of paints and cosmetics. But thereafter Hindenburg counted himself a Junker landowner; and he turned against Brüning the moment that he was persuaded that Brüning's plans threatened the great estates. On May 29th, 1932, Brüning was summarily dismissed.

With the dismissal of Brüning there began eight months of intrigue and confusion, in which the old order in Germany, which had now come into its own, struggled to escape from the conclusion that, to achieve its ends, it must strike a bargain with the gangsters of National Socialism. Fragments of past policies were resurrected haphazard, as a dying man recalls chance echoes of his life. First device was the Roman Catholic cavalry officer, Papen, and his "cabinet of barons," a collection of antiquarian conservatism unparalleled since the days of Frederick William IV, the sort of government which might have existed for a day if a few romantic officers had refused to acknowledge the abdication of William II in 1918. Papen's great achievement in the eyes of the Prussian landowners was to end constitutional government in Prussia: the Socialist ministers were turned out without a murmur. It was both curious and appropriate that Prussian constitutionalism, which had originated in the Junkers' selfish interest in the *Ostbahn*, should owe its death to the Junkers' selfish interest in the *Osthilfe*. Papen, in his daring, blundering way, continued, too, Brüning's undoing of Versailles, and accomplished the two decisive steps: reparations were scrapped in September 1932; German equality of armaments recognized in December. But it was impossible for a government of frivolous aristocrats, which would have been hard put to it to survive in 1858, to keep Germany going in 1932. Even the Centre, with its readiness to support any government, dared not offend its members by supporting Papen and expelled him from the party. The Germans, divided in all else, were united against the "cabinet of barons."

The army was forced to the last expedient of all: it took over the government itself. In December, Papen in his turn was ordered out of office and succeeded by General Schleicher, forced into office by his own intrigues. Schleicher, too, intended to do without the National Socialists, though he had often flirted with them in the past. He was the first professional soldier to rule Germany without an intermediary since Caprivi. Like Caprivi he was a "social general," intelligent enough to see the advantages of an alliance between the army and the Left, not intelligent enough to see its impossibility. To win over the Social Democrats, he revived the proposal for agrarian reform in eastern Germany and proposed to publish the report of the Reichstag committee on the *Osthilfe* at the end of January; in return he asked the trade union leaders to stand by him in his quarrel with the National Socialists. The prospect of the publication of the *Osthilfe* report made the Junkers around Hindenburg abandon all caution. The agent of reconciliation between the conservatives of the old order and the demagogic National So-

cialists was none other than Papen, who now hoped somehow to manoeuvre himself into the key position of power. Papen not only swung the Junkers behind Hitler. Early in January 1933 he negotiated an alliance between Hitler and the great industrialists of the Ruhr: Hitler was to be made Chancellor; the debts of the National Socialists were to be paid; and in return Hitler promised not to do anything of which Papen or the Ruhr capitalists disapproved. Papen's sublime self-confidence had already landed him in many disasters; but even he never made a more fantastic mistake than to suppose that Hitler's treachery and dishonesty, immutable as the laws of God, would be specially suspended for Franz von Papen. Against this combination Schleicher was helpless. He could not even count on the support of the Reichswehr; for though the army leaders had often acted independently of the Junkers and sometimes gone against them in great issues of foreign policy, they were not prepared to become the agents of agrarian revolution. They returned to the union of generals and landowners from which Bismarck had started. The *Osthilfe* report was to be published on January 29th. On January 28th Schleicher was dismissed and publication held up; and on January 30th Hindenburg, a field-marshal and a Prussian landowner, made Hitler Chancellor.

It was a symbolic act. The privileged classes of old Germany — the landowners, the generals, the great industrialists — made their peace with demagogy: unable themselves to give "authority" a popular colour, they hoped to turn to their own purposes the man of the people. In January 1933 the "man from the gutter" grasped the "crown from the gutter" which Frederick William IV had refused in April 1849. The great weakness of the Bismarckian order, the weakness which caused its final liquidation in January 1933, was that the interests of the "national" classes could never correspond to the deepest wishes of the German people. It was the Centre and the Social Democrats, not the Conservatives and still less the National Liberals, who had gained mass support. There was no need for a new party or a new leader to carry out the wishes of the landowners and the industrialists; but there was need for a new party and a new leader who would capture the mass enthusiasm, formerly possessed by the Centre and the Social Democrats, for the "national" programme. This was Hitler's achievement, which made him indispensable to the "national" classes, and so ultimately their master. He stole the thunder of the two parties which even Bismarck had never been able to master. The sham Socialism of his programme captured the disillusioned followers of the Social Democrats; the real paganism of his programme rotted the religious basis of the Centre.

There was nothing mysterious in Hitler's victory; the mystery is rather that it had been so long delayed. The delay was caused by the tragic incompatibility of German wishes. The rootless and irresponsible, the young and the violent embraced the opportunity of licensed gangsterdom on a heroic scale; but most Germans wanted the recovery of German power, yet disliked the brutality and lawlessness of the National Socialists, by which alone they could attain their wish. Thus Brüning was the nominee of the Reichswehr and the enemy of the republic, the harbinger both of dictatorship and of German rearmament. Yet he hated the paganism and barbarity of the National Socialists and would have done anything against them — except breaking with the generals. Schleicher, in control of the Reichswehr, was obsessed with German military recovery; yet he contemplated an alliance with the trade unions against the National Socialists and, subsequently, paid for his opposition with his life. The generals, the judges, the civil servants, the professional classes, wanted what only Hitler could offer — German mastery of Europe. But they did not want to pay the price. Hence the delay in the National Socialist rise to power; hence their failure to win a clear majority of votes even at the general election in March 1933. The great majority of German people wanted German domination abroad and the rule of law at home, irreconcilables which they had sought to reconcile ever since 1871, or rather ever since the struggles against Poles, Czechs, and Danes in 1848.

In January 1933 the German upper classes imagined that they had taken Hitler prisoner. They were mistaken. They soon found that they were in the position of a factory owner who employs a gang of roughs to break up a strike: he deplores the violence, is sorry for his work-people who are being beaten up, and intensely dislikes the bad manners of the gangster leader whom he has called in. All the same, he pays the price and discovers, soon enough, that if he does not pay the price (later, even if he does) he will be shot in the back. The gangster chief sits in the managing director's office, smokes his cigars, finally takes over the concern himself. Such was the experience of the owning classes in Germany after 1933. The first act of the new dictators won the game. When the terror of their private armies looked like failing, the National Socialists set fire to the Reichstag, proclaimed the discovery of a Communist plot, and so suspended the rule of law in Germany. The Reichstag fire, burning away the pretentious home of German sham-constitutionalism, was the unexpected push by which the old order in Germany, hesitating on the brink, was induced to take the plunge into gangster rule. The new Reichstag, still, despite the outlawing of the Communists, with no clear National Socialist majority, met under open terror. Hitler asked for an Enabling Bill, to make him legal dictator. He was supported by the "national" parties, and the Centre, faithful to its lack of principles to the last, also voted for Hitler's dictatorship, in the hope of protecting the position of the Roman Catholic Church; impotent to oppose, they deceived themselves with the prospect of a promise from Hitler, which was in fact never given. Only the Social Democrats were loyal to the republic which they had failed to defend and by a final gesture, impotent but noble, voted unitedly against the bill. But even the Social Democrats went on to show the fatal weakness which had destroyed German liberties. When in May 1933 the Reichstag was recalled to approve Hitler's foreign policy, the Social Democrats did not repeat their brave act: some abstained, most voted with the National Socialists. This was an absurdity. If Germany intended to undo the system of Versailles, she must organize for war, and she could organize for war only on a totalitarian basis. Only by renouncing foreign ambitions could Germany become a democracy; and as even the Social Democrats refused to make this renunciation the victory of the National Socialists was inevitable.

This is the explanation of the paradox of the "Third Reich." It was a system founded on terror, unworkable without the secret police and the concentration camp; but it was also a system which represented the deepest wishes of the German people. In fact it was the only system of German government ever created by German initiative. The old empire had been imposed by the arms of Austria and France; the German Confederation by the armies of Austria and Prussia. The Hohenzollern empire was made by the victories of Prussia, the Weimar republic by the victories of the Allies. But the "Third Reich" rested solely on German force and German impulse; it owed nothing to alien forces. It was a tyranny imposed upon the German people by themselves. Every class disliked the barbarism or the tension of National Socialism; yet it was essential to the attainment of their ends. This is most obvious in the case of the old "governing classes."

The Junker landowners wished to prevent the expropriation of the great estates and the exposure of the scandals of the *Osthilfe;* the army officers wanted a mass army, heavily equipped; the industrialists needed an economic monopoly of all Europe if their great concerns were to survive. Yet many Junkers had an old-fashioned Lutheran respectability; many army officers knew that world conquest was beyond Germany's strength; many industrialists, such as Thyssen, who had financed the National Socialists, were pious and simple in their private lives. But all were prisoners of the inescapable fact that if the expansion of German power were for a moment arrested, their position would be destroyed.

But the National Socialist dictatorship had a deeper foundation. Many, perhaps most, Germans were reluctant to make the sacrifices demanded by rearmament and total war; but they desired the prize which only total war would give. They desired to undo the verdict of 1918; not merely to end reparations or to cancel the "war guilt" clause, but to repudiate the equality with the peoples of eastern Europe which had then been forced upon them. During the preceding eighty years the Germans had sacrificed to the Reich all their liberties; they demanded as reward the enslavement of others. No German recognized the Czechs or Poles as equals. Therefore every German desired the achievement which only total war could give. By no other means could the Reich be held together. It had been made by conquest and for conquest; if it ever gave up its career of conquest, it would dissolve. Patriotic duty compelled even the best of Germans to support a policy which was leading Germany to disaster. . . .

German History Did Not Make Nazism Inevitable

EUGENE N. ANDERSON

THE GERMANS accepted National Socialism as a last act of desperation. A nation which appreciated its own excellent qualities and high abilities thought its existence menaced by chaos. It could not understand the reason for this plight and refused to acquiesce. Millions of Germans from all classes and occupations felt the crisis to be so acute that the Nazis were quickly transformed from a small group of crackpots into a mass party led by a messiah determined upon action to restore the vigor and the rightful glory of the German people. The ingredients of National Socialism were derived in sufficient strength from the German past to be acceptable as German. The *Führerprinzip* enjoyed the traditional prestige of centuries of absolute or strong monarchism, of Bismarckian authoritarianism, and of the traditions and habits of military and even bureaucratic command. It had been practiced, in an appropriate form, by Krupp, Stumm, and many other big industrialists. The new popular element in it was exalted as a sign of democratic equality and became immediately a powerful asset accepted even by the upper classes. The Germans also knew that in every crisis among every people the executive head becomes increasingly important as the instrument for quick and effective action. The relegation of parliament to an insignificant position seemed necessary and was fully approved by the millions of conservatives who had never liked representative government and by the middle classes and even many of the workers who cared less about it than about steady employment. Responsible representative government had had a short history, from 1919

to 1933, and had scarcely been crowned with success. The Germans were accustomed to a wide range of government authority, and in the crisis the individual wished the state to take even more responsibility away from him. The absence of tradition of private initiative and responsibility in civic affairs among most of the people and the dislike of politics and political parties as degrading influences led them to reject the potentialities of the Weimar Republic in favor of the wild promises of Nazism. They lacked democratic safeguards in the habits and standards of their private lives against the enticement of a seemingly easy way out of an unexpected and overwhelming crisis like that of the world economic depression. Certainly for some years until the destructive qualities of Nazism became apparent, few manifested any interest in defending moral principles against the nihilism of the National Socialist.

The qualities which German tradition regarded as the highest virtues became means of totalitarian domination. The Germans made a fetish of order, cleanliness, performance of duty, efficiency in craft or profession, concentration on the business in hand without interference in affairs about which they knew little, being obedient to officers and officials and to the law irrespective of the validity or morality of the order, ardent love of the nation and supreme loyalty to it. All peoples of our civilization have these traits in varying degrees, but in Western democracies they are balanced by a strong sense of civic responsibility and of individual worth as a citizen. In no other country than Germany did

From Gabriel A. Almond and others, *The Struggle for Democracy in Germany* (Chapel Hill, 1949), pp. 28–32. Reprinted by permission of the University of North Carolina Press.

such a combination of qualities obtain on such a broad scale, qualities which in favorable circumstances could be exploited to the ruin of a people.

One important line of German political and social philosophy for at least a century and a half had been basically concerned with the problem of the relation of the individual and the state. Scholars and popular writers at all levels of intelligence had discussed the subject. It permeated the cheap pamphlet literature which Hitler read as an embittered, unemployed ex-soldier. At times of prosperity the rights of the individual might be emphasized; but at every period of crisis — the Napoleonic era, 1848, the 1860's, the Bismarckian era, World War I, the economic depression of 1930–31, the Nazi seizure of power — the belief in the subordination of the individual to the welfare of the nation-state became widespread. This exaggeration seems logical and understandable for a crisis situation where the individual finds no way to solve his problems alone and throws himself upon the mercy of the state. The view forms the core of nationalistic thought in every country, France, England, Italy, Russia, Germany, or any other. It is the peculiar fate of German history, however, that the idea, derived easily from a class society struggling to maintain hierarchy, suited nicely the needs of the upper classes, especially the monarchy and the aristocrats, in their effort to keep control over the rest of the population. Since they dominated, or believed that with a little more action they could restore their domination over the lower classes, they kept alive the ideal of the superior interests of the state over those of the individual.

When National Socialism arose, it adopted for its own purposes this rich tradition. For the first time in history a nation sought to organize and run itself according to the ideals of nationalism. The process of nationalism which characterized European history after the French Revolution thereby reached its culmination. As stated above, the National Socialists could have found most of their ideals in the nationalistic writings of any country; there is nothing peculiarly German in them. No other people, however, has attempted to realize these ideals, for in no other country has the combination of conditions, inherited and present, been comparable to that which gave National Socialism its opportunity. Only one further step is possible in the unfolding of nationalism and of authoritarianism. That step may be described as national bolshevism. Although one strong faction wished to go so far, the National Socialists were unable to force the German people into the final act of destruction of their social and institutional heritage.

It would be wrong to conclude that Nazism grew inevitably from the German past. This theory would imply a fatalism which is entirely out of place in any serious study of history. A careful analysis of the events of 1932–33 shows that at that time a substantial majority of the German people favored an extraordinary increase in governmental authority necessary to solve their problems but opposed National Socialism, that this majority was increasing, and that the recession of the economic crisis would have entailed further losses of Nazi popular support. A relatively small group of Junkers, industrialists, and militarists actually achieved Hitler's appointment as Chancellor and utilized the senility of President von Hindenburg to accomplish its purpose. The group expected to control the Nazis and to exploit the Nazi power for its own purposes; but the National Socialists proved too clever and too ruthless for it, giving the next twelve years their own imprint. It would also be wrong to equate the conservative authoritarianism of the Hohenzollerns, Bismarck, the Junkers, the big industrialists, and the army officers with National Socialist authoritarianism. The conservatives believed in and practiced authoritarianism as a means of preserving their social, economic, and political status, a status quite different from that of Nazism. Their way of life included respect for at least some of the Christian virtues and for the qualities of their own type of cultured personality. It implied a certain reasonableness and a disinclination on the whole to run desperate risks. Perhaps one may counter by asserting that totalitarianism in all its fulness and with its extreme ruthlessness lay dormant in these groups and awaited the utilization of a Hitler. The growing evidence does not bear out this accusation. Rather it points to a milder view that these conservatives sympathized strongly with a popular totalitarian movement, the full import of which they did not understand, that their nationalism and their craving for power induced them to take a chance with Hitler, and that the authoritarian forms of their own thinking and acting and of those of the German people made possible the easy acceptance of National Socialism. The obedience of the German conservatives and all other elements to the Nazis through twelve years of hell does not prove the identity of all the German people with National Socialism. It merely reveals how politically irresponsible two generations of conservative authoritarianism had left a great nation and how susceptible the people were to nationalistic and military success, how unable they were to distinguish between a form of authoritarianism in the old Christian tradition which might have helped to solve their problems without violating the ideals and standards of Western culture and the violent, sadistic ultra-nationalism of Nazi nihilism.

Few Germans seemed to regret the disappearance of freedom after 1933. The overwhelming majority of the population either joyfully accepted dictatorship or acquiesced in it. While history helps to explain this fact, it also offers the assurance that the Germans have not always approved authoritarianism, that they have not always been nationalistic, indeed, that a large percentage opposed vigorously the Hohenzollern authoritarianism and militarism and preferred the ideals of freedom. History shows that on several occasions the adherents to freedom were powerful enough almost to gain a decisive victory. Historical conditions differed markedly in Germany's development over the past century from those of Britain and France and produced the peculiar mixture of elements from the *ancien régime,* modern industrial capitalism, and mass social movements which reached its fullest authoritarian form in National Socialism. History offers the assurance that under new and favorable conditions the Germans have the elements of a liberal and even democratic tradition of sufficient strength to encourage and assist them in turning toward democracy. There is no historical reason to doubt that they are able and would be willing to learn the ways of living in social and political freedom; but it is equally clear that their experience since national unification does not offer them much positive guidance. Conservative authoritarianism provides no assurance against a resurgence of totalitarianism. The fate of the Weimar Republic demonstrates that democracy depends upon more than a free constitution and free political instruments; it must permeate likewise individual conduct and social relations. It is this conception of democracy that the Germans must for the first time and on a national scale learn how to practice. . . .

A NATIONAL UPRISING AGAINST UN-GERMAN POSTWAR FORCES

The Nazis claimed that Jews and Communists made the revolution of 1918 and thus "stabbed the German army in the back." This *Dolchstoss* theory, although less than half true, was believed by millions of Germans after 1919. In the first selection in this unit, Léon Poliakov writes about Nazism's use of anti-Semitism as a political weapon. He is exceedingly well qualified to do so. Basing his coolly analytical writing upon the rich collections of sources at the Centre de Documentation Juive Contemporaine in Paris, M. Poliakov has published a number of books on the history of French, Italian, German, and other European Jews in the Nazi era. Translated into English as *Harvest of Hate,* his *Bréviaire de la Haine* is a thorough examination of Nazi anti-Semitism in the period 1933–1945. The second reading in this section is from a book by Milton Mayer, an American newspaperman. Himself a Jew of German descent, Mayer after World War II became intimately acquainted with ten former Nazis and got their life stories. In the second selection here, Mayer lets one of his ten Nazi "friends" (who never suspected that he was a Jew) tell how he and others turned to Nazism out of a desire to combat Communism.

Anti-Semitism: Cause or Result of Nazism?

LÉON POLIAKOV

I T IS a notorious fact that a virulent, ruthless anti-Semitism formed an integral part both of the ideology and of the practice of German National-Socialism, and did much, in fact, to give it its peculiar stamp. The outrageous form it took, as well as its far-reaching and dramatic consequences, tend to make it seem an end in itself ("extermination of the Jews"), whereas a closer analysis, such as we invite the reader to embark on now, shows that it was essentially a means towards the general ends envisaged by National-Socialism.

And two points should be established at the outset:

1. From the ideological viewpoint, the Nazi doctrine was almost entirely devoid of originality; it confined itself to systematising, codifying, and spreading certain views and conceptions, which were in existence long before the Third Reich.

2. From the practical viewpoint, on the other hand, when National-Socialism came to apply these ideas, it introduced certain fateful and disconcerting innovations, em-

From Maurice Baumont, John H. E. Fried, Edmond Vermeil, and others, *The Third Reich* (New York, 1955), pp. 832–836. Reprinted by permission of Frederick A. Praeger, Inc.

ploying methods and techniques which were both characteristic and novel.

But at this point we must look at the historical background.

I

When Hitler came to power in January 1933 he was at the head of Germany's most powerful Party, which, in the elections in July 1932, had gained more than 37 per cent of the total votes; in the 1933 elections he gained 44 per cent of the votes. All the other national and jingoistic parties and groups had already, some time before, given ground to National-Socialism and were virtually eliminated from the political stage. The hold National-Socialism had gained over the mass of the German population was due to the unrivalled effectiveness of Nazi propaganda, which worked in depth and had been in operation without a break for thirteen years. The basic principles of this propaganda were outlined with remarkable frankness by the *Führer* himself in *Mein Kampf:*

The receptive capacity of the mass of the people is very limited, their intelligence is small, but their faculty for forgetfulness is very great. In the light of these facts, any effective propaganda must confine itself to a small number of important points and use them as slogans ["*schlagerartig*"], till everyone understands the intended meaning. . . . The great majority of people have feminine traits and reactions, and it is not sober reflection but sensations and feelings that determine thoughts and actions. Feelings which, far from being complex, are concise and simple. They contain few nuances but a positive [side] or a negative [side], love or hate, justice or injustice, truth or lie. . . . No propaganda can be successful unless it takes into account a basic principle: to confine itself to a few things and repeat them incessantly. . . . Then one is amazed by the tremendous, inconceivable results such consistency achieves. . . .

Mein Kampf was written by Hitler during his detention in Landsberg prison in 1923–24. A few months later, in one of the first speeches he made after his release, he returned to the same theme with particular emphasis:

To make the great mass of the population understand a campaign, it must be directed against two objectives: against a person and against a thing.

Against whom was England fighting? Against the German Kaiser as a person and against militarism as a thing.

Against whom are the Jews fighting with the help of their Marxist power? Against the *bourgeoisie* as a person and against capitalism as a thing.

Against whom must we therefore fight? Against the Jew as a person and against Marxism as a thing.

And Hitler added:

For a people like the German people, it is particularly necessary to indicate one sole enemy, to march against one sole enemy.

According to this doctrine, then, the support of the masses could be gained only by confronting them with a single enemy, who, on the one hand, is absolutely bad and hateful, but, on the other hand, is tangible and accessible. This is an elementary principle of all demagogic propaganda. But it fell to Hitler to push it to its ultimate conclusion with an astonishing sequence of ideas. It is not important for this study (nor is it relevant) to know at what point the *Führer* and his lieutenants added faith to the both simple and intoxicating ideas which they took upon themselves to blazon abroad. On the other hand, once the principle is established that an incarnation of Evil must be chosen, it is important to show why this particular choice was made and why it had to be the Jew in preference to any other objective.

Let us first recall the peculiar situation of the Jews in European history. In medieval Christian society they were the only non-Christian confession: and mass antagonism to them found expression all the more readily in a violent, aggressive hostility because, in accordance with the teachings of the Church, they were also, traditionally, the deicides: a people, so to speak, that was criminally defective, condemned by its own transgression to perpetual servitude. In the period of the Crusades, in particular, a period of great mass exaltation and warlike fervour, popular agitators, adding to this standard accusation a series of circumstantial grievances (plague-spreading, well-poisoning, ritual murders, etc.), launched massacres and large-scale exterminations. In this way the Jews came to play, in history, the dreadful role of scapegoat on whom every form of social hatred was concentrated (and it is this very relentless hostility which, by a reverse reaction, forced Judaism to draw still more closely together, a fact which undoubtedly explains how they managed to survive throughout the ages and to maintain their religious and national identity). The gradual secularisation of European societies from the eighteenth century onwards, the apparent triumph of the Age of Reason, seemed, for one brief moment, to change the problem completely and to pave the way — this, at least, was what Christians and Jews hoped in all good faith — for the adjustment or assimilation of the Jews to the society around them, and thus put an end to the traditional hatred. But this hatred appears to have been too deep-rooted in the minds of the European peoples, for anti-Jewish passions flared up again in the twentieth century in a new form, the main difference being that, in keeping with the prevailing trends of the period, they fell back this time on science, in the shape of anthropological and racial doctrines, to provide them with ideological arguments and proofs. Such was the birth of modern anti-Semitism, a social plague that left few countries untouched, and that took a particularly virulent form in time of crisis.

It is not our task to investigate why the phenomenon in this form was at its most intense in Germany. Suffice it to say that if, in countries like Czarist Russia, it was, to a large extent, an instrument of government policy, artificially cultivated by the régime, and finding expression in a special legislation, in Imperial Germany, where the Jews benefited in principle from the equality of rights, it affected large masses of the population, but above all the *élites*. It was in Germany, around 1873, that the term "anti-Semitism" was coined; it was in Germany that race theories (first evolved in the main by Count Gobineau, a French aristocrat) were most laboriously interpreted and commented upon and most enthusiastically embraced, radiating beyond national frontiers and, in particular, towards the "brilliant satellite" Austria. Before the 1914–18 war Germany was the only European country in which *social discrimination*, that characteristic form of modern anti-Semitism, was systematically and openly practised in the army, and in state service in particular. And the picture of the Jew as a source of unrest and evil-doing, a ferment of decomposition and a poisoner of peoples, the opposite of this parasite being the frank, honest Aryan, a noble warrior or productive worker — a picture such as Hitler is to paint — is already becoming crystallised in people's minds with the works of H. S. Chamberlain (*The Foundations of the Nineteenth Century*) or the propaganda of Stöcker, chaplain of the Imperial Court: in this respect the *Führer* had invented nothing new.

One of the after-effects of the shock caused by the First World War was a marked revival of anti-Semitism in many countries. It is characteristic that the fable of "The Elders of Zion," first circulated fifteen years before by agents of the Czarist *Okhrana*, was seriously discussed at this time for several months in the columns of the British Press, including *The Times*. But Germany, defeated and disrupted, was infected in a special way, in proportion, one might say, to the extent of the disaster, of the traumatism inflicted on this proud nation. What a relief for many an embittered soul to be able to ascribe the cruel reality to the systematic activity of hidden forces, of a mysterious factor, of a secret, maleficent power! As early as 1919 a pornographic pamphlet by a certain Dinter entitled *The Sin against the Blood* (it appeared in 1911, but for a time remained almost unnoticed) reached a circulation of 600,000 copies. The former *élites* in particular, ruling circles and officers without pay, adopted the anti-Semitic line all the more easily because the Weimar Republic, which they hated so much, provided the unusual and shocking spectacle of Jews occupying high positions in administration and political life. Symbolic of this state of affairs is Ludendorff, the fallen marshal who became the exponent of a curious demonological doctrine, according to which mysterious "supra-state" powers (Jews, Jesuits, Freemasons) were responsible for Germany's misfortunes (and for the misfortunes of humanity as a whole). Out of this arose the *"Bund für deutsche Gotterkenntnis"* of the Ludendorffs; there were, of course, many other similar small groups, each expounding its own particular version of the original.

Such, then, was the ground on which the seeds of Hitler's propaganda fell, and it explains why his extreme anti-Semitism

had every chance of success. Once certain vague, latent preconceptions had been stirred up by methods prescribed in *Mein Kampf,* they promised to become unusually dynamic. In the circumstances then prevailing there seems to have been no other objective in Germany so appropriate as an incarnation of the enemy as the Jew.

But while Adolf Hitler, as we have pointed out, had nothing new to offer in the way of ideas and concepts, when it came to implementing and applying them, he immediately produced some revolutionary innovations, a study of which will enable us to look more closely at certain important characteristics of totalitarianism. And let it be recognised at once that these innovations, which in the early days of National-Socialism met with a certain amount of criticism and resistance even from nationalistic and anti-Semitic circles, were ultimately responsible for much of its success. As one German author, M. Müller-Claudius, puts it, the *Führer's* main task is to transform "state hate" into "dynamic hate." . . .

Communism as a Cause of Nazi Popularity

MILTON MAYER

IT HAD its beginning in Munich," said my Friend Herr Kessler, the one-time Catholic from Bavaria's neighboring state of Württemberg in southern Germany. . . .

"The situation in Germany got worse and worse. What lay underneath people's daily lives, the real root, was gone. Look at the suicides; look at the immorality. People wanted something *radical,* a real change. This want took the form of more and more Communism, especially in middle Germany, in the industrial area, and in

the cities of the north. *That* was no invention of Hitler; *that* was real. In countries like America there is no Communism because there is no desire for *radical* change.

"Hitlerism had to answer Communism with something just as radical. Communism always used force; Hitlerism answered it with force. The really absolute enemy of Communism, always clear, always strong in the popular mind, was National Socialism, the *only* enemy that answered Communism in kind. If you wanted to save

From Milton Mayer, *They Thought They Were Free: The Germans, 1933–1945* (Chicago, 1955), pp. 95–97. Reprinted by permission of the University of Chicago Press.

Germany from Communism — to be *sure* of doing it — you went to National Socialism. The Nazi slogan in 1932 was, 'If you want your country to go Bolshevik, vote Communist; if you want to remain free Germans, vote Nazi.'

The middle parties, between the two millstones, played no role at all between the two radicalisms. Their adherents were basically the Bürger, the bourgeois, the 'nice' people who decide things by parliamentary procedure; and the politically indifferent; and the people who wanted to keep or, at worst, only modify the status quo.

"I'd like to ask the American Bürger, the middle-class man: What would *you* have done when your country stood so? A dictatorship, or destruction by Bolshevism? Bolshevism looked like slavery and the death of the soul. It didn't matter if you were in agreement with Nazism. Nazism looked like the only defense. There was your choice."

"I would rather neither," I said.

"Of course, Herr Professor. You are a bourgeois. I was, too, once. I was a bank clerk, remember."

Of my ten friends, only two, Tailor Schwenke and Bill-collector Simon, the two *alte Kämpfer*, wanted to be Nazis and nothing else. They were both positive — still are — that National Socialism was Germany's and therefore their own, salvation from Communism, which, like the much more sensitive bank clerk, they both called "Bolshevism," "the death of the soul." "Bolshevism" came from outside, from the barbarous world that was Russia; Nazism, its enemy, was German, it was their own; they would rather Nazism.

Did they know what Communism, "Bolshevism," was? They did not; not my friends. Except for Herr Kessler, Teacher Hildebrandt, and young Horstmar Rupprecht (after he entered the university, in 1941), they knew Bolshevism as a specter which, as it took on body in their imaginings, embraced not only the Communists but the Social Democrats, the trade-unions, and, of course, the Jews, the gypsies, the neighbor next door whose dog had bit them, and his dog; the bundled root cause of all their past, present, and possible tribulations. . . .

A TOOL OF CRISIS CAPITALISM

It was not a combination of "Versailles and Moscow" that caused the Nazi movement, contends Franz Neumann. It was rather "the imperialism of German monopoly capital." George W. F. Hallgarten essentially agrees with this point of view. The first reading in this section is by Neumann, who was a noted labor economist in Germany before the Nazi revolution. He taught for many years at Columbia University prior to his untimely death in an automobile accident in 1954 in Europe. The reading is from the best known of Neumann's several books on German affairs. George W. F. Hallgarten is a vigorous American scholar of German-American parentage. The author of several books, he is especially well known for his two-volume study, *Imperialismus vor 1914* . . . (Munich, 1951). The ideas expressed in the second reading in this section are developed more fully in his study, *Hitler, Reichswehr und Industrie* . . . (Frankfurt, 1955).

The Crisis of German Capitalism

FRANZ NEUMANN

THE STRONG man of the Social Democratic party, Otto Braun, Prussian prime minister until 20 June 1932 when he was deposed by the Hindenburg-Papen *coup d'état*, attributes the failure of the party and Hitler's successful seizure of power to a combination of Versailles and Moscow. This defense is neither accurate nor particularly skilful. The Versailles Treaty naturally furnished excellent propaganda material against democracy in general and against the Social Democratic party in particular, and the Communist party unquestionably made inroads among Social Democrats. Neither was primarily responsible for the fall of the Republic, however. Besides, what if Versailles and Moscow had been the two major factors in the making of National Socialism? Would it not have been the task of a great democratic leadership to make the democracy work in spite of and against Moscow and Versailles? That the Social Democratic party failed remains the crucial fact, regardless of any official explanation. It failed because it did not see that the central problem was the imperialism of German monopoly capital, becoming ever more urgent with the continued growth of the process of monopolization. The more monopoly grew, the more incompatible it became with the political democracy. . . .

The efficient and powerfully organized German system of our time was born under the stimulus of a series of factors brought into the forefront by the First World War.

From Franz Neumann, *Behemoth: The Structure and Practice of National Socialism* (Toronto, New York, and London, 1942), pp. 14–16, 30, and 34. Reprinted by permission of the Oxford University Press.

The inflation of the early '20s permitted unscrupulous entrepreneurs to build up giant economic empires at the expense of the middle and working classes. The prototype was the Stinnes empire and it is at least symbolic that Hugo Stinnes was the most inveterate enemy of democracy and of Rathenau's foreign policy. Foreign loans that flowed into Germany after 1924 gave German industry the liquid capital needed to rationalize and enlarge their plants. Even the huge social-welfare program promoted by the Social Democracy indirectly strengthened the centralization and concentration of industry, since big business could far more easily assume the burden than the small or middle entrepreneur. Trusts, combines, and cartels covered the whole economy with a network of authoritarian organizations. Employers' organizations controlled the labor market, and big business lobbies aimed at placing the legislative, administrative, and judicial machinery at the service of monopoly capital.

In Germany there was never anything like the popular anti-monopoly movement of the United States under Theodore Roosevelt and Woodrow Wilson. Industry and finance were of course firmly convinced that the cartel and trust represented the highest forms of economic organization. The independent middle class was not articulate in its opposition, except against department stores and chains. Though the middle class belonged to powerful pressure groups, like the Federal Union of German Industries, big business leaders were invariably their spokesmen.

Labor was not at all hostile to the process of trustification. The Communists regarded monopoly as an inevitable stage in the development of capitalism and hence considered it futile to fight capital concentration rather than the system itself. Ironically enough, the policy of the reformist wing of the labor movement was not significantly different in effect. The Social Democrats and the trade unions also regarded concentration as inevitable, and, they added, as a higher form of capitalist organization.

Their leading theorist, Rudolf Hilferding, summarized the position at the party's 1927 convention: "Organized capitalism means replacing free competition by the social principle of planned production. The task of the present Social Democratic generation is to invoke state aid in translating this economy, organized and directed by the capitalists, into an economy directed by the democratic state." By economic democracy the Social Democratic party meant a larger share in controlling the monopolist organizations and better protection for the workers against the ill effects of concentration.

The largest trusts in German history were formed during the Weimar Republic. The merger in 1926 of four large steel companies in western Germany resulted in the formation of the *Vereinigte Stahlwerke* (the United Steel Works). The *Vereinigte Oberschlesische Hüttenwerke* (the United Upper Silesian Mills) was a similar combination among the steel industries of Upper Silesia. The *I. G. Farbenindustrie* (the German Dye Trust) arose in 1925 through the merger of the six largest corporations in this field, all of which had previously been combined in a pool. In 1930 the capital stock of the Dye Trust totaled 1,100,000,000 marks and the number of workers it employed reached 100,000.

At no time in the Republic (not even in the boom year of 1929) were the productive capacities of German industry fully, or even adequately, utilized. The situation was worst in heavy industry, especially in coal and steel, the very fields that had furnished the industrial leadership during the empire and that still dominated the essential business organizations. With the great depression, the gap between actual production and capacity took on such dangerous proportions that governmental assistance became imperative. Cartels and tariffs were resorted to along with subsidies in the form of direct grants, loans, and low interest rates. These measures helped but at the same time they intensified another threat. The framework of the German government was still a parliamentary democracy after all, and what if movements threatening the established monopolistic structure should arise within the mass organizations? As far back as November 1923, public pressure had forced the Stresemann cabinet to enact a cartel decree authorizing the government to dissolve cartels and to attack monopolistic positions generally. Not once were these powers utilized, but the danger to privileges inherent in political democracy remained and obviously became more acute in times of great crisis. . . .

Even before the beginning of the great depression, therefore, the ideological, economic, social, and political systems were no longer functioning properly. Whatever appearance of successful operation they may have given was based primarily on toleration by the anti-democratic forces and on the fictitious prosperity made possible by foreign loans. The depression uncovered and deepened the petrification of the traditional social and political structure. The social contracts on which that structure was founded broke down. The Democratic party disappeared; the Catholic Center shifted to the right; and the Social Democrats and Communists devoted far more energy to fighting each other than to the struggle against the growing threat of National Socialism. The National Socialist party in turn heaped abuse upon the Social Democrats. They coined the epithet, November Criminals: a party of corruptionists and pacifists responsible for the defeat in 1918, for the Versailles Treaty, for the inflation.

The output of German industry had dropped sharply. Unemployment was rising: six million were registered in January 1932, and there were perhaps two million more of the so-called invisible unemployed. Only a small fraction received unemployment insurance and an ever larger proportion received no support at all. The unemployed youth became a special problem in themselves. There were hundreds of thousands who had never held jobs. Unemployment became a status, and, in a society where success is paramount, a stigma. Peasants revolted in the north

while large estate owners cried for financial assistance. Small businessmen and craftsmen faced destruction. Houseowners could not collect their rents. Banks crashed and were taken over by the federal government. Even the stronghold of industrial reaction, the United Steel Trust, was near collapse and its shares were purchased by the federal government at prices far above the market quotation. The budget situation became precarious. The reactionaries refused to support a large-scale works program lest it revive the declining power of the trade unions, whose funds were dwindling and whose membership was declining. . . .

By joining the concert of the Western European powers the Weimar government hoped to obtain concessions. The attempt failed. It was supported neither by German industry and large landowners nor by the Western powers. The year 1932 found Germany in a catastrophic political, economic, and social crisis.

The system could also operate if the ruling groups made concessions voluntarily or under compulsion by the state. That would have led to a better life for the mass of the German workers and security for the middle classes at the expense of the profits and power of big business. German industry was decidedly not amenable, however, and the state sided with it more and more.

The third possibility was the transformation into a socialist state, and that had become completely unrealistic in 1932 since the Social Democratic party was socialist only in name.

The crisis of 1932 demonstrated that political democracy alone without a fuller utilization of the potentialities inherent in Germany's industrial system, that is, without the abolition of unemployment and an improvement in living standards, remained a hollow shell.

The fourth choice was the return to imperialist expansion. Imperialist ventures could not be organized within the traditional democratic form, however, for there would have been too serious an opposition. Nor could it take the form of restoration of the monarchy. An industrial society that has passed through a democratic phase cannot exclude the masses from consideration. Expansionism therefore took the form of National Socialism, a totalitarian dictatorship that has been able to transform some of its victims into supporters and to organize the entire country into an armed camp under iron discipline. . . .

German Industrialists Paid Hitler

GEORGE W. F. HALLGARTEN

Down to the time of the depression, the German bankers and the captains of industry had not shown much interest in sponsoring fascism or nazism proper. While hardly less eager to check communism than anybody else in the Reich, they felt they could do so most efficiently by continuing the policy of cooperation with the German trade unions which Hugo Stinnes, the later so-called "king of the Ruhr," and the union leader Carl Legien had inaugurated in the defeat-clouded autumn of 1918. To be sure, heavy industry and its affiliates had not always followed this line too meticulously. During the months of social radicalism which followed the outbreak of the German Revolution in November 1918 a group of the Reich's most prominent businessmen, comprising Stinnes, Albert Voegler (then director of the Gelsenkirchen Mining Co., Ltd.), Carl Friedrich von Siemens, Felix Deutsch (of German General Electric), Director Mankiewitz, of the Deutsche Bank, and Director Salomonsohn, of the Diskontogesellschaft, financed the movement of a Hitler forerunner, one Dr. Eduard Stadtler, who demanded the establishment of a German National Socialist state and who was instrumental in the smashing of communism in Berlin — then called Spartacism — and in the killing of its leaders, Karl Liebknecht and Rosa Luxemburg. In the Ruhr, Stadtler's movement was backed by the very same steel producers who, as will be shown, later backed Hitler: Emil Kirdorf, the venerated but dreaded God Wotan of German heavy industry, Albert Voegler, Fritz Springorum, of the Hoesch steel group, and also by Paul Reusch, of the Haniel group, and August Thyssen, father of Hitler's later financier Fritz Thyssen. But as soon as actual street fighting stopped, the industrialists dropped Stadtler and returned to their political cooperation with union labor.

Hitler who originally was nothing but the chief of an insignificant nationalist south German group could not hope to change this basic line followed by the Ruhr industrialists. Down to 1929 his party appears to have lived, in the main, on membership dues and individual gifts, mainly from local South German producers. A donation by Fritz Thyssen in 1923 remained an isolated fact. Even the party's increasing intimacy with Emil Kirdorf did not change the picture. A survivor of the period when the Reich, under Bismarck's leadership, had tried to solve the workers' question by a mixture of benevolent despotism and brutality, Kirdorf was consid-

From George W. F. Hallgarten, "Adolf Hitler and German Heavy Industry, 1931–1933," *Journal of Economic History*, XII (Summer, 1952), 223–232, 239–243, and 245–246. Reprinted by permission of the publisher, New York University Press.

ered out-of-date by everybody but the Nazis. Even the fact that he opened to the party access to the funds of the Bergbaulicher Verein and the Federation Eisen Nord West should not be overrated. Compared to the increasing indebtedness of the party which by 1933 rose to 70–90 million reichsmarks, these payments were only a drop in the bucket. For the same reason, it is not too important to determine the exact amount that Hitler received at this and other occasions, as even the highest figures mentioned remained far behind the party's expenditures. What mattered was the fact that such amounts came in at all. They were like shots in the arm which proved to the millions of Hitler's followers that their Führer was "in" with the right type of people and thus deserved credit, politically and economically. After 1929 Hitler's chances in both fields improved rapidly. Favored by the increasing depression and by the funds he received from Alfred Hugenberg, leader of the conservative German Nationalist party in the Reichstag, the chief of the Nazis managed to raise the number of Nazi voters within two years from 800,000 to far over 6 millions. The Reichstag elections of September 14, 1930, gave the Nazis 107 seats, which made them the second largest party. The following year, with its bank crashes and public scandals which led in the summer to the closing of the German stock exchange and to the establishment of currency control, widened the Nazis' chances of success. From this time on, Hitler had dozens of meetings with business leaders, to gain support.

The depreciation of the British currency, on September 20, 1931, made the situation of the German exporters desperate and caused heavy industry to formulate an antidepression program which it could hardly hope to carry through without some Nazi help. Acting in the name of all German employer organizations, the Reich Federation of German Industry demanded that public expenses be cut down, that salaries be lowered according to the international market situation, that the social-insurance expenditure, including the subsidies to the unemployed, be slashed, and that the mail and freight tariffs be reduced. During the following weeks heavy industry made an all-out attack against the weak Bruening cabinet. The nationalist meeting in Bad Harzburg in October, in which Hugenberg and Hitler participated, became an assembly center of the industrial leaders, with men like Dr. Hjalmar Schacht, the Hamburg shipbuilder Blohm, the steel merchant Ravené, the United Steel head Ernst Poensgen, and a trusted agent of the steel people, Schlenker, in attendance. The debates centered largely around the currency question. After a long inner fight, heavy industry, in view of its interest in purchasing raw materials cheaply and in saving the Reich's inner purchasing power, refrained from advocating a German currency depreciation, which Dr. Schacht appears to have advocated. But in other respects Schacht was successful. Since the end of 1930 a public supporter of Hitler, the former president of the German Reichsbank and weathervane of German economic policy opened Hitler's way to the big banks. To show his recognition, Hitler cut the last tie that connected him with Gottfried Feder, the economic quack who in bygone days had impressed him greatly, but whose agitation against the "interest slavery" did not fit into the spirit of those days. Schacht saw to it that Feder was given a successor as Hitler's adviser in economics in a man better meeting the wishes of the industrialists: it was Dr. Walter Funk, an economic journalist who later became minister of economics and whom the Nuremberg court sent to prison for life.

Funk's appointment, effected with the help of Gregor Strasser, symbolized the rising interest that leaders of heavy industry took in the party. The mining industry subsidized Funk's orientation bulletin, the *Wirtschaftspolitischer Dienst*, with several thousand reichsmarks a month. In the performance of his new duties, Funk worked in close connection with Schacht, Dr. von Stauss, of the Deutsche Bank und Diskontogesellschaft, Hermann Goering, and Goering's helpers and associates in this field, Directors Hilgard, of the Alliance Insurance Corporation and Curt Schmitt of the Munich Reinsurance Corporation as well as Dr. Lubert, of the Verkehrswesen Ltd. and of the big building firm, Lenz and Co., all of whom he introduced to Hitler. Schmitt later became Hitler's minister of economics.

Hitler was too good a politician, however, not to see the dangers which his ties with big business created both for his movement and himself. To be sure, he was not opposed to the making of profits by capitalist producers, as long as their ways did not cross his own. He felt, however, that his intended dictatorship called for the destruction of all elements of the existing society that could hamper his rule, comprising both union labor and all producers who refused to cooperate with him. The thought that his becoming a hireling of Hugenberg made him dependent on a type of businessman unwilling to accept his rule and the planned economy it involved drove him almost to physical despair. It is reported that during the Harzburg meeting in October 1931, when he was forced by the penury of his movement to co-operate with Hugenberg in a public demonstration, he showed signs of hysterical fury and behaved like an irresponsible madman. Before long, he took steps to break out of this ambiguous situation. "During a conversation which I had with the Fuehrer in December, 1931," Wilhelm Keppler relates, "the Fuehrer said: 'Try to get a few economic leaders — they need not to be Party members — who will be at our disposal when we come to power.'" This was the start of the so-called "Circle of Friends," the entering wedge of the Nazis into the ranks of heavy industry as a whole. Keppler, a depression-stricken small businessman who had become Hitler's agent in economic matters, states that the Führer mentioned no other names aside from Dr.

Schacht and, presumably, Albert Voegler, the director general of the United Steel Works, leaving it up to him, Keppler, to solicit members during the trips he took. He adds that in doing so he, Keppler, used the services of his distant relative, Kranefuss, a small industrialist like himself who was Heinrich Himmler's personal adjutant and who later succeeded in ousting him from the leadership of this group.

At the end of 1931 the results of this activity became gradually visible. In a New Year's article for 1932 Friedrich Reinhardt, director of the Commerz-und Privatbank, and one of the first nine members of the Keppler circle, launched a campaign for German economic self-sufficiency, a policy which spelled doom for the German consumers, merchants, and exporters but which was welcome to the producers of steel and coal and called for rearmament and imperialism, to make up for the sacrifices it involved. In the same days the press reported that Hitler had gained the support of Ludwig Grauert, the secretary general of the important Federation of German Employers, Group Northwest (Ruhr), who determined the attitude of heavy industry in wage questions. Grauert's attitude caused Schlenker, the executive secretary of the northwest German steel industry and of the so-called "Long Name Federation" (Federation for Safeguarding the Business Interests of Rhineland and Westphalia), to follow suit.

The big steel producers, during those days, clashed sharply with the steel-processing industry, since they no longer felt able to pay it the customary reimbursements for the price difference between the international and the inland prices for steel, in the case of exported steel goods. As the German steel prices were 214 per cent above the international level, this change in policy was a deadly blow to exporters. To maintain the domestic price level, heavy industry, facing sudden bankruptcy, started looking for public orders.

This general situation was the background for an event which Otto Dietrich later called decisive in the history of the movement: it was Hitler's speech in the Industry Club in Düsseldorf on January 27, 1932. Initiator of this meeting was Fritz Thyssen, next to Kirdorf the most prominent of Hitler's supporters in the ranks of the industrialists. A son of a stern and hard-working father who had founded one of the three largest privately owned industrial empires in the Ruhr, Fritz Thyssen, suppressed, unsteady, and errant, was the problem child of the Reich Federation of heavy industry and the target of ire of his workers, who hated the feudal manners of this overbearing and pleasure-loving magnate. Several decades younger than Kirdorf, who always remained a Bismarck admirer, Thyssen admired the last Kaiser. He hoped that Hitler would help the industrialists to re-establish the Wilhelmian regime. This being so, Thyssen took a certain pride in presenting Hitler to the greatest assembly of industrialists the later Führer had ever met. In his speech, Hitler as usual expressed his dissatisfaction with the Treaty of Versailles and with the democratic system and declared it to be his general aim to rearm Germany and to take affirmative action in order to achieve German objectives in foreign affairs. He stated that "Germany's power position . . . is . . . the condition for the improvement of the economic situation" and that "there can be no economic life unless behind this economic life there stands the determined political will of the nation absolutely ready to strike, and to strike hard." Otto Dietrich says that in this speech Hitler succeeded in breaking through the reserve of the western German captains of industry, and Thyssen expresses the view that the "speech made a deep impression on the assembled industrialists, and in consequence of this a number of large contributions flowed from the resources of heavy industry," a statement which seems somewhat exaggerated.

The day following the speech at the Industry Club, Ernst Poensgen and Albert Voegler met Hitler, Goering, and Roehm at Thyssen's castle, Landsberg. The con-

tent of their conversation is unknown. Poensgen states, however, that Goering asked the industrialists whether they would allow Ludwig Grauert, Hitler's newly won supporter, and head of the employers Organization Northwest, to become minister of labor in a Hitler cabinet.

In the person of Albert Voegler, Kirdorf's associate in the chairmanship of the Gelsenkirchen board, chairman of the Federation of German Steel Miners, and director general of by far the biggest German steel combine, the United Steel Works (Vereinigte Stahlwerke), Hitler met, not for the first time, the man who next to Kirdorf was the most representative figure of the German steel industry of those days and whose experience even a Thyssen could not match. An ardent nationalist and imperialist who in the First World War had headed the drive for the incorporation into the Reich of the French iron-ore basin of Briey and Longwy and who later financed Dr. Stadtler, Voegler supported the Nazis in the apparent hope of saving his combine from disaster by a policy of lowering wages, soliciting government orders, and sponsoring general rearmament. As already said, he was one of the two persons whom Hitler mentioned by name when urging Keppler late in 1931 to organize the Circle of Friends, the other man being Dr. Schacht, the close friend of Dr. von Stauss, of the Deutsche Bank und Diskontogesellschaft. What Hitler presumably did not yet know was the fact that Voegler's industrial combine, the United Steel Works, was threatened by a disaster similar to the one which in the summer of that year had overpowered the German banks and had forced the Reich to intervene and take over some of their functions.

Victims to a large extent of their own rationalization and price policy which created unemployment and prevented recovery, the Voeglers and Stausses expected to obtain salvation by endorsing a dictatorship that would spend for rearmament. In doing so, they inevitably provoked the ire and the bitter criticism of scores of other businessmen and producers who were not "in" with the big concerns and resented the latters' Nazism. This type of criticism later furnished one of the bases for the many misstatements and exaggerations by the defense in Nuremberg when it tried to prove that big business as a whole hated Hitler. In the weeks of January and February 1932 when Poensgen, Voegler, and the three top Nazis deliberated, Voegler, as will be shown presently, secretly notified the Reich bureaucracy, that the big steel combine he headed was facing disaster, unless supported by public means. His statements were made jointly with a man who from being a comparatively unknown little industrialist had reached, in those days, a position of great influence in German heavy industry: Friedrich Flick whom the Nuremberg tribunal later sentenced to seven years in prison for having committed crimes against humanity. Like Voegler, Flick too, considered co-operation with the Nazis to be one of the many ways that might lead him out of the disaster that was threatening him and all his allies. Through the initiative of Walter Funk he in February 1932 had a first interview with Hitler. None of these steps, however, had immediate success. Hitler, as was his habit, submerged his visitor in a torrent of words which prevented Flick from saying what he wanted. Besides Hitler, during those days, was hardly able to make definite promises which would have saved the steel magnates from disaster.

Having decided to run against old President von Hindenburg in the presidential elections, Hitler was not much less of a gambler than was a man like Flick. During the electoral campaign, he saw with dismay that the bulk of German industry still supported the German People's party, the comparatively moderate group once headed by the late Stresemann, which joined the parties of the Weimar Coalition in advocating Von Hindenburg's candidacy. To Hitler's anger, the opponents of his rule and advocates of co-operation with union labor still controlled the commanding posi-

tions of the German Republic and German industry. This basic situation did not change even after Reich President von Hindenburg, re-elected on April 10, 1932, in a hard fight at the polls against the self-styled Führer, turned his back on his voters, the Weimar parties and others, dismissed the Reich Chancellor, Dr. Bruening, and with the consent of Reichswehr and Nazis appointed a Junker-controlled cabinet, under Franz von Papen. While most of the measures envisaged by the new cabinet, such as the restriction of democratic liberties, the absorption of the jobless by public works and the suppression of the Weimar regime in Prussia corresponded to Nazi ideas, Hitler saw with mounting fury that the credit for this policy was going to men who were out to destroy him.

The entire year 1932 is marked by a series of efforts to carry out his program without giving him personal power and to use his party as a policeman in the interest of others. Champions in this game were first Reich Chancellor von Papen and his Junker cabinet and, after Von Papen's resignation in November, the Reichswehr leader, General Kurt von Schleicher. Since none of these men dared openly to violate the Constitution and, instead of governing without a parliament, resorted to the means of Reichstag dissolutions, the day of parliamentary reckoning was going to come sooner or later. But Hitler's unsuccessful running for Reich President, in the spring of that year, and the two consecutive Reichstag dissolutions that followed, loaded down his party with heavy debts, in the amount of 70–90 million gold marks, and made it highly improbable that, in the decisive moment, he would still be a political factor to reckon with. Recognizing the intentions of the Von Papen cabinet to wear him down and to make Junkers and heavy industry the sole masters of the Reich, Hitler during that entire eventful year was like a madman racing against time. . . .

The interest the United Steel group took in his cause enabled Hitler to overcome the party crisis of the fall of 1932, when the Nazis almost succumbed to the Von Papen policy of exhausting them by a series of expensive election campaigns. The party crisis even increased the aid the Nazis received from the steel group, since it coincided with a development that made them indispensable to the steel men. Down to November most producers, including even many of those who hoped for Nazi support, endorsed the cabinet of Von Papen who represented both Junkers and industrialists, and who tried to use the Nazis merely as a Frankenstein, in order to terrify the leftists in the Reichstag. Fortunately for the Nazis, the chancellor, since the fall of 1932, no longer had the support of the Reichswehr minister, General von Schleicher, whose intrigues early in the spring, had brought his cabinet into power. In November, Von Papen resigned and Von Schleicher took over the chancellorship. Unlike Von Papen, the general was more concerned with finding a mass basis for the increase of the army than with maintaining shaky class privileges. With grave anxiety Junkers and heavy industry witnessed the efforts made by Von Schleicher to come to an understanding with union labor and with the left wing of the Nazis, and to draft an anti-depression program which in every respect contradicted their wishes. While both Von Papen and Von Schleicher were agreed that the depression should be fought by public spending and an armament program, the general, distrustful of the military ambitions of leading Nazis, would have been happy if granted the backing of the Socialists in the Reichstag. This outcome would have deprived both Junkers and industry of the profits they hoped to reap from militarization, not to mention the danger many of them incurred by a Reichstag investigation of the Osthilfe matter or by a socialization of heavy industry based upon the Reich's ownership of the Gelsenkirchen shares. Thus Hitler, in the very last moment, when his party, weakened by three big election campaigns within eight months, was facing both bankruptcy and a catastrophic loss of votes, obtained the long-expected chance of presenting himself as the savior of society. He even was saved from financial distress by the very same circles that he was expected to save politically.

Still, heavy industry was far from giving the Nazis its unanimous and unqualified support. The independent producers, while deeply concerned over the Von Schleicher trend, feared the economic dictatorship of the men around United Steel much too strongly to fall in with their political wishes. Walter Funk's trip through the Ruhr late in 1932 to collect money for the party, became a dismal failure, the only major contribution being an amount of 20 to 30,000 reichsmarks given to him by Steinbrinck for Flick. Hardly more lucky than Funk in his efforts to help the Nazis was Otto Prince zu Salm-Horstmar, one of the old wirepullers of German economic imperialism who in the middle of October urged Gustav Krupp to sign an appeal — as it appears in favor of Nazi admission to the government — which had been decided on the day before by a small committee. After the November elections in which the Nazi vote sank to 33.1 per cent of the total votes as compared to 37.4 per cent in the elections of July 31, Curt von Schroeder, banker of the United Steel group, Albert Voegler, United Steel director, and Dr. Hjalmar Schacht approached the leading industrial circles with the request to sign a petition in which President von Hindenburg was urged to make Hitler chancellor. The response they found outside the circle of the United Steel group was not encouraging. Paul Reusch and Fritz Springorum of the Hoesch steel group informed Voegler that they agreed with the petition but did not desire to add their signatures. The same answer was given by the directors Kiep and Cuno, of the Hamburg-American Steamship Line. Dr. Schacht's report to Hitler on the progress of the campaign was couched in most careful terms. "Permit me to congratulate you on the firm stand you took," he wrote immediately after the elections. "I have no doubt that the present development of things can only lead to your becoming chancellor. It seems as if our attempt to collect a number of signatures from business circles for this purpose was not altogether in vain, although I believe that heavy industry will hardly participate, for it rightfully bears its name 'heavy industry' on account of its indecisiveness."

The Goebbels diaries of those weeks show most clearly how both the morale and the financial situation of the party, under these conditions, sank to an unheard-of low, and how the party was threatened with a split. Fortunately for Hitler, the moderate wing of big business which backed Von Papen was hardly less interested in preventing a complete downfall of the party than were the Nazi enthusiasts around the United Steel Works. Threatened with the Von Schleicher solution which involved a likely blow to both Junkers and big business as a whole, the Von Papen group, centered in the Herrenklub circle, was prepared to listen to compromise proposals made by its nazified colleagues. This is the background for the famous meeting between Von Papen and Hitler of January 4, 1933, in the house of the Cologne banker, Curt von Schroeder, the business associate and confidant of Voegler, Kirdorf, Thyssen, and Flick. "The general aim of the industrialists at that time," Von Schroeder later told allied interrogators who questioned him about his arranging this meeting, "was to see a strong leader come to power in Germany who could form a government which would long remain in power. When on the 6th of November 1932, the NSDAP suffered its first set-back and had thus passed its peak-point, the support of German heavy industry became a matter of particular urgency."

About his personal interest in bringing about a political turn which would help to make United Steel a going concern and prevent the socialization of the German steel industry, Von Schroeder in his various testimonies did not talk. The general picture, however, is obvious enough. Immediately after the Hitler-Von Papen meeting, which before the end of the month resulted in Von Hindenburg's appointing Hitler as Reich Chancellor, with Von Papen as vice-chancellor, a consortium of industrialists, headed by Voegler and Springorum and including many members of the Circle of Friends, gave Von Schroeder's bank, J. H. Stein, one million reichsmarks for distribution among the S. S. The consortium also saw to it, that the Nazi party's most urgent election debts were paid. Thyssen, to be sure, remained uninformed about the Cologne meeting but he had good reason to be happy about its outcome. To open his pro-Nazi activity Hermann Goering at that time called him up and told him that the communists planned his assassination. For German industry as a whole, the meeting of Cologne had far-reaching consequences which even outweighed the settling of the Gelsenkirchen matter as such.

Hitler's final rise to power became equivalent in the industrial field, to a victory of the steel producers and coal miners — Thyssen, Voegler, the Tengelmanns, Springorum, Knepper, Buskuehl — and of their allies in the insurance business and in the chemical industry such as Kellermann, Von Schnitzler, and Gattineau over the representatives of the big independent family enterprises, such as Krupp, Peter Kloeckner, Paul Reusch, of the Haniel-controlled Gute Hoffnungshütte, Hugo Stinnes, Jr., and Carl Friedrich von Siemens, the head of the famous Siemens electrical firm. It would appear that the old industrial families of the Ruhr feared Hitler's budding totalitarianism much more strongly than did the directors of the anonymous companies who live on big salaries, instead of on individual profits. . . .

Summing up, one might say that the big concerns which supported Hitler's rise to power consisted mainly of those groups which — more or less thanks to their own doing — had been hardest hit by the depression, and thus hoped for the coming of a "savior." Among these groups the big banks, some of which had collapsed in 1931, were conspicuous, since all of them faced the threat of socialization. In the Circle of Friends and other Nazi agencies, this group was represented by men like Friedrich Reinhardt, Emil Meyer, Emil von Stauss and, as their agent, Hjalmar Schacht. The other group, leading in industry, consisted of the United Steel Works circle which has been dealt with here at length. The rest of the big industrial concerns, while welcoming Hitler as an ally against labor, would have preferred to see him being used as a mere tool in the hands of a cabinet controlled by industry and Junkers. Even such ardent Hitler supporters as Thyssen would doubtless have been happier if Hitler, in the long run, had helped them to re-erect the monarchy instead of playing Kaiser himself. When this proved not to be feasible, however, they supported Hitler as the lesser of two evils, eager to make the best of his coming to power, both politically and economically. In this respect, all documentary sources concur, though many gaps remain to be filled, since the Nuremberg trial records which are our best available source of material were assembled for juridical rather than for historical needs.

While Hitler was strongly assisted by the industrialists' funds, one cannot say that industry "made" his movement. A movement of such enormous size as his which in 1932 controlled 230 seats in the Reichstag, is not made by any individual or group. It might be more correct to state that heavy industry by its very existence and social nature caused the movement, or, at least, helped to cause it and once it was given birth tried to use it for the industrialists' purposes. Mechanization and economic concentration, maintenance of monopoly prices and monopoly agreements, with the resulting pressure on small competitors, were the fertile ground on which mass fascism grew. In the period of Locarno and the following years this development was still counterbalanced by boom and employment. But in the depression years after 1929 it became suddenly apparent that the German middle class, in the postwar inflation, had lost the remnants of its economic independence. In Germany, the nation of military Prussia, the declining middle class was too strongly inspired by military and aristocratic ideologies to turn socialist or New Deal or to attack the existing society, with its unsound and obsolete agrarian structure, and its expansion-minded concerns. On the other hand, neither was it conservative. Deeply mistrusting the men in control of the command positions of German economy, it turned desperado and strengthened the power of a leader half a vagabond and half a policeman, half a slave and half a ruler, who, in the manner of a *condottiere,* offered the ruling classes "protection" against criminal punishment and labor troubles and, by a mixture of threats and blackmail, made himself master over both wealthy and poor.

PRODUCT OF THE PROMISE AND FAILURE OF SOCIALISM

Friedrich Meinecke was a world-renowned historian when Hitler came to power in 1933, and his opposition to Nazism was then already established. In 1935 he was removed from the editor's chair of Germany's most important journal of history, the *Historische Zeitschrift*, after having guided it masterfully for forty years. In 1946, while most fellow Germans were still in a state of shock, eighty-four-year-old Friedrich Meinecke sought to analyze the reasons for the success of Nazism in Germany. His book *Die Deutsche Katastrophe* (Wiesbaden, 1946), develops his thesis that the rise of moderate, democratic Socialism played an important part in conditioning the German people psychically for the acceptance of National Socialism, though democratic Socialists in 1932–1933 were Hitler's enemies. The first reading in this section is the major part of Meinecke's discussion of this question. A noted American historian, Sidney B. Fay, has called Meinecke's book "an object lesson in historical objectivity," and has translated it into English. The second reading in this section is by Gerard Braunthal, a political scientist at the University of Massachusetts. The article from which this reading is selected is based upon thorough study of the politics of German labor leaders in 1932–1933. Professor Braunthal has also written on the West-German labor movement since World War II.

Product of the Promise of Socialism

FRIEDRICH MEINECKE

THE QUESTION of the deeper causes of the frightful catastrophe which burst upon Germany will still occupy the coming centuries — provided these centuries are indeed still able and inclined to ponder problems of this kind. But then the question of the German catastrophe broadens at the same time to a question which extends beyond Germany to the destiny of the West in general. . . .

The whole bourgeois world [in the 1880's], whether anti-Semitic or pro-Semitic, was still borne along on one of the two waves which swept through the nineteenth century — the wave of the national movement. But this was crisscrossed, as has already been said, by the second great wave —the socialist movement which arose from the masses of the industrial proletariat. We shall limit ourselves here to the attempt to explain what this second movement, by its inherent tendencies as well as by its re-

From Friedrich Meinecke, *The German Catastrophe: Reflections and Recollections*, trans. by Sidney B. Fay (Cambridge, Mass., 1950), pp. 1, 16–19, 25, 70–72, and 111.

action upon the bourgeois world, may have meant for the rise of National Socialism.

The socialist state that was the goal of the future could be realized only as a state which was to a high degree authoritarian and which organized daily life thoroughly. It remained at first a dream of the future and the thinking of the masses was certainly more concerned with the needs, cares, and desires of daily life than with it. One may suspect, however, that it helped materially to collectivize the masses and to modify deeply their feeling about legal rights; that is, the rights of the individual grew dimmer and the rights of the total state over the individual were allowed to become continually stronger. The phrase "prison state" was flung in reproach at the socialists because that described, so it was said, what they were trying to set up. On the other hand, the anger and hate of those who felt exploited toward the other traditional social groups, who were regarded as reactionary, directly undermined the feeling for traditional historical authority in general. Hatred inflamed the revolutionary recklessness with which people trampled upon the rights and property of their opponents. So there developed a revolutionary spirit in general, to which National Socialism could later fall heir. The thing that was astonishing and characteristic of German development was the fact that this revolutionary spirit could change its bearers and could somehow leap from the class of the industrial proletariat, which had carried it hitherto, to other social classes now arising, some for the first time. We shall speak later of this process.

Within the Social Democratic range of ideas, however, alongside of the long-prevailing revolutionary solution of the problem of the future, there was also another *evolutionary* solution. It counted on a gradual, step-by-step amelioration and transformation of the social situation and on successes, small at first but cumulative, in the struggle of the workers against the capitalist world. The goal of a completely new reordering of the social world was not thereby abandoned, but was pushed off into the distant future.

Such "revisionist" ideas, to be sure, could begin to prevail over orthodox revolutionary Marxism only after actual developments toward the turn of the century had become favorable to them. Not increasing misery, as the revolutionary theory demanded, but a perceptible improvement of the standard of living of the German working classes took place. And no longer was there *one* mass of all the other classes interested in capitalism standing in hostile opposition to them. The formerly integrated opposition was loosened as it was caught in the stream of development: a part was quite willing to make concessions to the workers and another part was quite hardened in its determination to fight any threatening revolution with the most determined reaction. The evolutionists in one camp found justification and support in the evolutionists of the other camp, and the rank revolutionists found an echo and to a certain extent a historical counterpart in the rank reactionaries. Such was the general course of the interaction of the two great waves of the bourgeois national movement and of the proletarian socialist movement. Let us make this clear in detail.

The evolutionary side of the story rests on two basic facts, one purely economic, the other resulting from a combination of political, social, and moral factors. The purely economic fact was the tremendous economic upsurge since the nineties, which brought well-being and wealth to the bourgeoisie, and also gradually brought better wage opportunities and a slow rise in the standard of living to the workers. Even before this upsurge, an idea of social reform existed in the state and among the bourgeoisie. It took practical shape in the social security insurance legislation during the eighties toward the close of the Bismarck era. Among the bourgeoisie there was an agitation in various quarters to carry this social reform further and make it even more effective. In the nineties Friedrich Naumann took the most radical lead in this

matter through his national socialist movement which had as its organ the magazine
Hilfe (Help).

Let us look at the deeper historical significance of this movement. It demanded
for the future the merging together in a
powerful union of the two great waves, the
bourgeois-national and the proletarian-
socialist. Such a union was, as we said at
the outset, highly desirable and even vital
for the entire nation because in both waves
a deep and justifiable ferment which could
be historically fruitful was at work. For
these waves to continue ever crisscrossing
and interfering with each other could not
remain the last word in their history. In
each of the waves, however, there was also
a tendency to mount too high, to be dangerously one-sided. If the union was to be
successful, there had to be moderation in
each of the movements; they had to be
united somehow at the point where what
was harmful in each did not get the upper
hand.

Now Naumann's attempt, though it was
greeted with great enthusiasm by the German bourgeois and idealistically inclined
youth, did not succeed, as is well known,
in bringing about a union of the two waves
—that is, in bringing the bourgeoisie and
the working classes into harmony in regard
to the great basic questions of public life.
Had Naumann been successful, there probably would never have been a Hitler
movement. . . .

It was one of the noblest dreams in German history, but a dream which came at a
time, partly too early and partly too late,
to be actually realized. However, the little
which it did accomplish ought not to be
unduly undervalued. One can see that before the First World War the Naumann
movement, even after it had failed as an
independent political party, helped to create bridges and possibilities of understanding between the bourgeoisie and the
working classes. It encouraged and spiritu-
ally enriched the revisionist movement
within Social Democracy. In the exaltation
and feeling of brotherhood during the

August days of 1914 there lay something
of the ethos and pathos of Naumann's
dream. . . .

When the First World War broke out,
it seemed once more that a kind angel
might lead the German people back to the
right path. The exaltation of spirit experienced during the August days of 1914, in
spite of its ephemeral character, is one of
the most precious, unforgettable memories
of the highest sort. All the rifts which had
hitherto existed in the German people, both
within the bourgeoisie and between the
bourgeoisie and the working classes, were
suddenly closed in the face of the common
danger which snatched us out of the security of the material prosperity that we had
been enjoying. And more than that, one
perceived in all camps that it was not a
matter merely of the unity of a gain-
seeking partnership, but that an inner ren-
ovation of our whole state and culture was
needed. We generally believed indeed that
this had already commenced and that it
would progress further in the common experiences of the war, which was looked
upon as a war of defense and self-protec-
tion. We underwent a rare disappointment
in our hopes. Within a year the unity was
shattered and the German people were
again separated upon various paths. . . .

The historical question now arises, however, whether this Hitler experiment was
really, as its lamentable outcome seems to
indicate, ruinous in all its aspects. Was it
not after all borne along by a higher historical necessity, which must certainly be
called tragic because it ended in disaster,
but which, nevertheless, contributed perhaps fruitful ideas that were more than
mere weapons in the battle for power? If
so, such ideas, even after the downfall of
those who held them, might retain some
value, whether by perpetuating the memory of a gigantic heroic resolve, or by their
own practical survival in new forms of
effort.

This question, whether Hitler's thousand-year Reich contained valuable and
viable elements, not for a thousand years,

to be sure, as he imagined, but just perhaps for our own century, occupied many persons otherwise opposed to him during the twelve years of oppression. The many fortune-seeking opportunists who supported him were very zealous in giving an affirmative answer to this question. But it is also a political and historical duty of conscience to pass judgment on one's own self and on one's own former ideals and to test as far as possible without prejudice the new ideals that were offered to us Germans. The underlying Satanism that rose to heights along with the ideals certainly ought never to be forgotten. But what great, new, existence-changing idea is there in which Satan has not insinuated himself both as driver and as beneficiary! How horrible to us seems the attempt made once before in Germany to found a thousand-year reign, the reign of the Anabaptists in Münster in 1535. Yet that Anabaptist movement in general contained seeds of great fruitfulness for religion and for ways of looking at the world.

We recall what we said at the beginning: the pressure exerted on all existence by the increased masses of population; arising from this pressure, the two waves, nationalist and socialist, of the nineteenth and twentieth centuries the way the waves crisscrossed and worked upon each other and finally strove to unite. If this union had succeeded, new and unsuspected forms of life might have grown out of them. Friedrich Naumann's proposals, rich in ideas, were an initial theoretical attempt in the direction of this union. They failed because the ideal prerequisites broke down before the coarser mentality and the selfish egotistical group-interests of the conflicting political parties and social groups. But Naumann's attempt survived nevertheless in the work of the Weimar Republic, to which Naumann always remained true and to which he devoted his last strength. His idea survived, to be sure only in a weakened form, moderately and without brilliance, in the necessary Weimar Constitution, over which lay the heavy weight of

the Versailles Treaty. Added to all this was the depressing picture of a parliamentary system gone to seed and choked with weeds; the quarrels of lesser officials at the formation of every new cabinet; and finally the scandals of corruption which certainly were immeasurably exaggerated by the Hitler propaganda. Brüning was undoubtedly on the way toward creating a firm governmental authority at the center of the state by strengthening the presidential power. But whatever success he had in this contributed only to his own downfall. Hindenburg would scarcely have dared in the earlier years to have dismissed a chancellor who was opposed by no parliamentary majority. Hitler, however, apparently offered much stronger remedies for all the ills and needs of the time. And the big idea that was floating in the air — the idea of the amalgamation of the nationalist and socialist movements — unquestionably found in him the most ardent spokesman and the most determined practitioner. His share in this great objective idea must be fully recognized.

Hitler wanted to overtrump the bourgeois, class-egotistical nationalism of his heavy-industry patrons and money providers, and also the Marxism of the Russian bolshevists, which he attacked with special zeal and which wanted to condemn the bourgeoisie to extinction. He therefore seized upon the idea that the creation of a new fruitful folk community need not rest upon the one-sided victory of the one or the other of the social forces contending against one another — that the natural groupings of society did not have to be unceremoniously destroyed — but that they must be steered around and educated to serve a community which included them all. Hitler's undertaking seemed to promise more continuity with the traditions and values of the existing bourgeois culture than the radical new edifice of bolshevism. With this idea he bribed a wide circle of citizens. The working class, he intended, should be inspired with the full pride that their productive work merited and thereby lose all their inferiority complexes which sprang from the beginnings of the class struggle. The same fundamental idea of nurturing the special pride of the professional classes and amalgamating them with the all-embracing community was also extended to the peasantry. There was no lack of specious enticements for all classes — celebrations, festivals, and so forth. . . .

The reason that Hitler's National Social-ist experiment was so unsound was that it threw into the mixing pot the national element only in its most frightful form of a degenerate and unbridled nationalism and a racial madness. As a result, the socialist element that was thrown in from the other side was denatured and robbed of its best content. . . .

The Failure of Socialist Labor

GERARD BRAUNTHAL

A DEMOCRATIC nation, especially if faced with powerful extremist forces of the political Left and Right, ought to have a free and dynamic trade union movement to help safeguard the liberties of its citizens. For the sake of survival alone, labor not only should make its members aware of the political problems of the day, but also should participate in those national and international affairs which affect its broader interests. If the movement in an hour of political crisis withdraws from this participation, there is grave danger that it will be unable to resist the onslaughts of totalitarianism. This is precisely what happened in Germany in 1933. Therefore, it seems appropriate to make a case study of the attitudes and policies of the German free trade unions during the crucial period of transition from the Weimar Republic to fascism.

Three independent and competing organizations represented organized labor in Germany at the end of the nineteenth century. These were based on ideological and political differences. The Socialist unions adhered to the concept of Marxist revisionism, the Christian unions to Catholic social action and the Hirsch-Duncker unions to Manchester liberalism. Of the three, the Socialist unions were by far the largest and politically the most active. Consequently, this article will be concerned only with these unions. By the end of the Weimar period, they had become constituent members of three national federations working in close cooperation: (a) the German Federation of Trade Unions, ADGB (*Allgemeiner Deutscher Gewerkschaftsbund*), composed of national industrial and craft unions, with a membership of nearly 5 million; (b) the Free Federation of Salaried Employees, AFA (*Allgemeiner freier Angestelltenbund*), with almost 500,000 members; and (3) the German Federation of Civil Servants, ADBB (*Allgemeiner Deutscher Beamtenbund*), numbering approximately 170,000 members.

The three federations, representing about twenty-five per cent of the total labor force, were closely allied with the Social Democratic Party (SPD or Party) and rather consistently espoused its aims. Unlike American organized labor at that time, the

From Gerard Braunthal, "The German Free [Socialist] Trade Unions during the Rise of Nazism," *Journal of Central European Affairs*, XV (January, 1956), 339–353. Reprinted by permission of S. H. Thomson and Gerard Braunthal.

German unions were committed to political parties and directly involved in the affairs of the nation. German labor upheld the democratic regime on many occasions, and most notably at the time of the right wing Kapp Putsch in 1920 when a prompt general strike call contributed to the failure of the uprising. It must be emphasized that for the most part both the members and leaders of the "free" unions were Socialists and staunch opponents of the Communists and Fascists.

Yet, when democracy was threatened in the latter period of the Weimar Republic, the movement had lost its élan and was close to paralysis. With the Depression organized labor confronted crucial problems: unemployment had risen steeply, and the economic survival of the nation was at stake. Was it not, however, important also that labor realize the danger of pursuing a politically sterile and negative course of action in the face of imminent danger to the organization as well as to the nation?

In order to understand the attitudes which actually prevailed and the decisions which were made, the role played by the Socialist unions during the authoritarian régimes of von Papen, von Schleicher and Hitler must be reviewed.

THE PAPEN COUP

On July 20, 1932, Chancellor Franz von Papen dramatically ousted the legitimate Prussian coalition government headed by Otto Braun, Social Democrat. The conservative Chancellor held no brief for Socialists and trade unionists. On the pretext that law and order were not being preserved in Prussia, long a stronghold of the Socialists, Papen had himself appointed Commissioner for Prussia by Presidential decree. Then, on the broad authority given him, he dismissed the eight Prussian cabinet ministers, who forthwith appealed to the Supreme Court, on the grounds that an outright dismissal of ministers by federal decree was unconstitutional. But it was too late. The court decision, generally in their favor, was not rendered until October

25, when it could no longer be of significance. This coup d'état undoubtedly was one of the chief factors in bringing about the rise of fascism, and was the first of numerous illegal acts performed by irresponsible German governments.

How did the Socialist trade unions react to Papen's dramatic move? On the part of the rank and file, the response was an immediate work stoppage in a few plants, followed by a pause for instructions. Berlin workers in the sprawling Siemens and I. G. Farben plants assembled to hear their leaders speak. Small formations of the Iron Front, a semi-military, Socialist-led defense organization, gathered in various sectors of Berlin to wait for directions. But no call for a general protest strike or even a token demonstration came from their chiefs.

The ADGB Board and Executive met immediately on the afternoon of the 20th and decided not to take any action. Their reasons were similar to those voiced by SPD leaders on the following day: unemployment and increasing defeatism among the workers rendered immediate action impracticable, but cautious preparations for a possible future general strike should be made. A spokesman for the Railroad Workers Union claimed that his men had no wish to strike as many unemployed workers were ready to step into their jobs. Also, reportedly, it was argued at the meeting that Papen had acted within the limits of his constitutional powers and that consequently the unions must reject any strike call.

The SPD called on its Executive Committee and Board members to attend an emergency meeting in Berlin on July 21. At this conference it was decided to bring all organizations to a state of readiness, but to refrain from immediate action. Three main considerations led to these decisions: the hope that the July 30 election, then ten days off, would turn the tide against fascism by increasing the vote for the Left; the desire at all costs to avoid a civil war, with the Reichswehr fighting the workers; and the belief that Papen was still attempting to prevent Hitler's assumption of power. The SPD moreover rejected the proposal of the Communist Party for a general strike, declaring that, in view of the collaboration between Communists and Nazis in a plebiscite against the Prussian government the previous year, it preferred to act on its own.

Once immediate action was ruled out, Otto Wels, Party Chairman, systematically sounded out trade union, Party and Iron Front leaders on the feasibility of future resistance. Fearing bloodshed, they responded negatively. The Chairman of the Frankfurt trade union council, Otto Misbach, in a typical reply to the query, categorically refused to engage in any "experiments" which were doomed to failure. The spokesman of the Metal Workers Union and Reichsbanner [Socialist militia] Council in Frankfurt, Mulanski, declared that the Reichsbanner did not even have sufficient equipment at its disposal to transport workers to a possible scene of action.

The Iron Front* Executive members also held a caucus at which most Party and Union spokesmen stressed their fear that an immediate general strike would lead to civil war. They decisively rejected a proposal by Karl Höltermann, head of the Reichsbanner, and Siegfried Aufhäuser, AFA President, that, at the very least, a demonstration strike be held.

Though the no-strike decision reached at the three meetings was revealed without delay, it was followed by supplementary declarations. On July 20 and 21, the Berlin locals of the national unions issued two appeals warning workers of *provocateurs* who, in the name of the Iron Front and without authorization, were agitating for a general strike. The appeals asked the workers to follow only the legitimate union leadership. Another official declaration asserted that, despite the excitement of the workers, exemplary discipline must be

maintained, especially since no solution could be reached in Prussia until the Supreme Court had rendered its decision. These releases once more clearly demonstrated that labor was not ready to risk a civil war, but preferred to await developments. The first setback to the Party and Union occurred on July 31, when the National Socialists registered further gains in the nation-wide election, thus becoming an increasing menace to the fragile structure of the Weimar Republic.

In retrospect, whether the no-strike decision was the correct one remains a matter of debate. Had the trade unions decided on a general strike or token demonstration, the Party would have backed them up. Conversely, the Party could not possibly have initiated a strike with the unions opposing it. Which organization made the original decision remains a moot question, although all indications are that the unions were primarily responsible.

Certain differences in political outlook within the Party and within the Union which were never overcome in the Weimar period stood out clearly in the 1932 crisis. As the danger of fascism grew, the ideological split between the minority who wanted more militant action and the majority who feared any hasty action was intensified within each organization.

Whatever one may have thought of the feasibility of calling a general strike, the decision of the Union and the Party not to act weakened any hope of further resistance to fascism. Symptomatic of the passive mood of the two organizations was their refusal even to consider a demonstration strike to rally the masses. Thus the only major forces available at that critical hour which could perhaps have saved the deteriorating situation failed to make the attempt.

THE SCHLEICHER RÉGIME

General Kurt von Schleicher, Reichswehr leader and War Minister in the cabinet of von Papen, succeeded his chief as Chancellor on December 3, 1932. Before

---

* In 1931, the Reichsbanner, a Social Democratic defense organization, and other groups jointly set up the para-military Iron Front to combat the enemies of democracy.

forming the cabinet, Schleicher, who lacked an organized party following of his own, considered different combinations of the various political and trade union groups.

One plan called for the creation of a labor government led by German generals. Apparently, Schleicher believed that such a coalition would prevent the rise of Hitler. But, of course, no such collaboration was possible then since the two groups had no basis for agreement. The General reportedly also toyed with a Rightist combination of the Reichswehr, allied with Papen, Göring, and Hitler, but the Nazi chiefs refused to enter into any cabinet in which Schleicher would be chancellor. In another move, the General held conversations with the "moderate" group of Nazis headed by Gregor Strasser and with the trade union leaders, in an attempt to reconcile the major social forces. He intended to split the Nazi movement by offering Strasser the twin posts of vice-chancellor and Prussian prime-minister, but the negotiations crumbled when Strasser's prestige and mass support in the Nazi Party declined.

In his parleys with organized labor, Schleicher seemed to have short-range and long-range goals in mind. He often expressed the hope in private conversations that all trade union organizations would sever their links with the political parties, unite in one labor front, and counteract the Nazi menace by exercising more power in the state. He also envisioned the eventual organization of the economy into guilds, and the institution of a corporative government based largely upon the trade unions.

With some of these goals in mind, Schleicher paid compliments to ADGB President Theodor Leipart at a Berlin assembly of works council representatives in October, 1932. On November 28, five days before he assumed the chancellorship, Schleicher invited Union representatives to a personal conference. Their acceptance, however, aroused particular controversy in some Party and labor circles where it was feared that the Union would make a deal with the General.

Gustav Noske, former SPD War Minister, describes in his memoirs an episode which supposedly occurred immediately after Schleicher's request for such a conference came to the notice of the SPD Executive members. "At once Leipart was asked to come to Party headquarters. . . . There Breitscheid told him that the Party rejected any collaboration with reactionary Schleicher, and expected the same attitude from him (Leipart). Leipart, who described this conversation to me, yielded to the Party pressure." The conversation nevertheless took place. Leipart and Wilhelm Eggert, Union heads, participated and, as reported by the official Union and Party organs, stressed the need to initiate an employment policy and render void Papen's unpopular wage-slashing decree of September 5. Schleicher asked Leipart to submit these demands to him on the following day in written form. According to another source, the General made a favorable impression on Leipart and Eggert at the meeting when he told them that Papen had donated too much money to Prussian Junker estates, and that Papen's wage cuts were too drastic. The two labor leaders thereupon dropped their demands for socialization of key enterprises, but demanded a large public works program as a condition for supporting Schleicher.

After several days of negotiations with the various parties and trade union organizations, Schleicher finally formed his cabinet on December 3, retaining, with only two exceptions, the same conservative ministers who had served under Papen. The SPD and other parties, for conflicting reasons, did not support the new government, which thus rested on precarious foundations. . . .

Papen's backstage intrigues and pressures forced Schleicher to resign on January 28, 1933. Two days later, President Hindenburg administered the oath of office to the new Chancellor, Adolf Hitler, who, ironically enough, promised to uphold the Constitution. January 30 proved to be a fateful day in German history. It marked the definite end of the Weimar period and the beginning of the fascist era.

Would the unions undertake any last-minute move to rescue the nation, or yield to the fascist assumption of power? We know that they chose the latter path, and failed again to use their most potent weapon, the general strike. There were many diverse excuses given for this lack of action: it was pointed out that the Chancellor had assumed his office legitimately, and that the odds were against the workers, since any uprising would be crushed by the Reichswehr. It was argued later that the unions could not yet discern the totalitarian character of the fascist movement, that they believed Hitler would not remain long in power, and that they could hope to save themselves from extinction by ending the collaboration with the Party.

There was apathy among all ranks of labor, caused partly by the failure of the leaders to present any positive plan for counteracting the Nazi policies. The Union might have advanced an effective anti-depression program of deficit financing, as was practiced by the United States "New Deal" and the Swedish labor governments in the 'thirties. It might have rallied the workers to a political program of broad scope; it might have demanded, for instance, that the major democratic parties bury their differences and unite against the Right. But by now it was too late. A general strike would undoubtedly have led to civil war, and the Union leaders were not willing to risk it. . . .

In its declarations, the Union characteristically asked the workers to remain calm and to follow the slogan of the hour: "Organization, not demonstration." It still entertained hope for the future and asserted that even the new government would not be able to crush the workers and their unions. In line with the policy during the Schleicher administration, the Union announced that it intended, despite its opposition to the government, to present the demands of the workers to the nation's leaders.

The ADGB Board, on January 31, issued a carefully worded statement, in which it was implied that, if necessary, a compromise in order to conform with government policies might be accepted. The Board argued that while the desire of the workers to take action against the new administration was understandable, such a step would merely harm their interests. Governments are transitory, it was emphasized, and reactionary ones do not necessarily destroy the labor movement. While this release was issued in order to preserve the organization, it nevertheless left no doubt about the passive mood of the ADGB staff officials and their mistaken appraisal of the new régime.

During the month of February, it is true, there was hope that the unions would stand firm. They protested Nazi chief Göring's order to the police, SA and SS (Nazi semi-military units) to unite against the Left, but were ignored. Furthermore, some union speakers urged SPD and KPD (Communist Party) workers to bridge their differences and unite. In Berlin, Clothing Workers and Lithographers Unions asked the ADGB to seek an agreement between the SPD and the KPD, but the ADGB took no action, for it had already decided a year earlier that it would not put its weight behind a unity campaign until the KPD stopped attacking the socialist unions and the SPD.

Despite the formal Union appeal to its members to vote for the SPD in the March 5 nation-wide election, the next two months, March and April, gave rise to indications that the Union, in order to preserve itself, was beginning to adopt a neutral political attitude. In a letter to the right wing SPD leader Wilhelm Keil, dated March 3, Leipart categorically asserted that he intended to remain in the political limelight no longer, and hoped that organized labor would now benefit from his earlier modest role in the activities of the Party.

After the March 5 Nazi election victory, gained as a result of a wave of terror against all opposition parties, the AFA

Executive (Federation of Salaried Employees) drew up a resolution which stated in part:

It cannot be the task of the trade unions to take a stand on the political consequences of this election. However, (they) . . . are cognizant of their duty to continue to work for the fulfillment of their social and economic task in this historic, significant moment for the country and its people.

Ten days later, the ADGB Executive issued a document of great importance, which was similar in content to the AFA resolution. The ADGB declared that a trade union must be independent of political parties as well as of employers. Its social tasks must be fulfilled no matter what government is in power, but it should not attempt to interfere directly in politics.

Following these official declarations, most local labor weeklies urged their readers not to voice political opinions but to devote their time entirely to economic problems. In a similar vein, the ADGB journal declared that the Union was more than ever occupied with its immediate tasks, and that the reduced political role of the workers must be balanced by strengthening the organization.

These policy declarations did not have the desired effect. Hopes of saving the movement crumbled when the Nazis increased their relentless persecution of the unions, thereby causing much hardship. The many-pronged attack was carried out against the property of the unions, their leaders and press, and the newly-elected officials of the works councils.

The attacks on union property constituted flagrant violations of democratic procedure. On March 8, the ADGB training school in Bernau was occupied by SA men. The ADGB Executive immediately protested to Vice-Chancellor Papen and Prussian Commissioner Göring, who had the building cleared and returned to the Union. Renewed Nazi attacks on union property prompted further protests. On March 10, the ADGB appealed to the President to stop the infringements of the law, the acts of terror against union members, and the destruction of property. The appeal was in vain. More headquarters were occupied or closed by the police, labor leaders were arrested, and it was decreed in many German states that no union official could hold a party office or agitate against the government.

In another type of crackdown, the Nazis periodically confiscated and suppressed labor newspapers. This caused the newspapers to exercise great caution in their comments on Hitler's speeches to the Reichstag and on other Nazi pronouncements.

The government brazenly dismissed from office ADGB candidates successful in the works council elections. Once again, the Union appealed to the administration, but received no satisfaction. It was belatedly realizing that its efforts were becoming increasingly futile.

There was no unanimity in labor ranks regarding the policy that should be pursued as a result of the illegal Nazi acts. In a book of doubtful reliability, Hermann Seelbach, head of the ADGB training school of minor union functionaries, and secretly a Nazi Party member, reveals that among his students there was as little agreement as at the top level. A large group favored yielding to the Nazis (an attitude prompted by Seelbach himself), a second smaller group counseled a "let us wait and see" attitude, and only a small group advocated illegal anti-Nazi action. The groups engaged in constant discussions on the future role of the unions, but the decision was not in their hands; it rested with the Union Executive. Yet, at Executive meetings the debates merely centered on methods of countering individual Nazi attacks. Broader issues and policies were rarely touched upon, according to Seelbach, chiefly due to the lack of knowledge of government plans.

Apparently the majority of Union leaders, partly under the influence of Seelbach and other minor chieftains, who later revealed themselves as NSDAP members, did favor a compromise with the Nazis. Accordingly, at the demand of the ADGB, Professor E. R. Huber, an associate of Hitler's advisor Carl Schmitt, drafted a document on the future legal position of the organization. It recommended the recognition of the unions in the state and, simultaneously, their transformation into public legal bodies by a coordination (*Zuordnung*) with the Third Reich.

The unions also attempted to clarify their precarious position by engaging in discussions with Nazi representatives. Since Minister of Labor Seldte and other conservative cabinet members no longer held any influence over Hitler, the unions were forced to negotiate directly with the National Socialist Shop Organization (NSBO). A conference was thereupon held on April 5 between leading ADGB and NSBO staff officials. NSBO chief Bruckner took the initiative. He outlined the Nazi program, and revealed that the government intended to form a unitary labor organization, headed by an appointed leader, and would regulate wages and prices. Bruckner asked for the resignation of the ADGB President. Labor officials Leipart, Grassmann, Eggert, and Leuschner retorted that the unions had fought a valiant struggle in the past to obtain their goals, and could not agree to the arbitrary appointment of a new leader. Leipart refused to resign from his post, still under the illusion that he could save the unions from extinction.

On March 28, a week before this conference, the AFA Executive gave indications of yielding to the government by evolving reorganization plans. On April 6, however, the ADBB Executive (Federation of Civil Servants) agreed to disband its organization before any further administration measures would crush the labor movement. The ADGB continued its precarious existence, even though its leaders, once active in the SPD or in the international labor movement, were resigning.

The methodical pressure on organized labor increased. The government decreed that May First, a holiday traditionally celebrated by the forces of the Left, would be a "National Labor Day." Apparently, this was a calculated Nazi maneuver to win the allegiance of the workers to the fascist state. Simultaneously, plans were made to crush the free labor movement the day after the celebration. NSDAP chief Joseph Goebbels records that on April 17 he discussed with Hitler plans for May Day and the seizure and occupation of trade union buildings on May 2. Goebbels foresaw the possibility of a few days of struggle.

On April 15, the ADGB Executive asserted that it welcomed the government's May Day decision. The declaration left up to the members the question of whether to participate in the official demonstrations. After pressure reportedly was exerted by other trade union organizations, the ADGB Board issued a declaration on April 19 requesting the members to participate "for the honor of creative labor, for the complete incorporation of the working masses into the state." The manifesto represented a clear-cut capitulation to the fascist government, and was followed by the Nazi-sponsored May Day demonstrations.

A few columns appeared in the official Union journal which compromised even with the Nazi ideology. In its final issue, an article welcomed the May Day and the "socialist" principles embodied in National Socialism. The article read in part:

We certainly need not strike our colors in order to recognize that the victory of National Socialism, though won in the struggle against a party which we used to consider as the embodiment of the idea of socialism (SPD), is our victory as well; because, today, the socialist task is put to the whole nation.

Even this last desperate effort to save the Union failed completely. For the Nazis, a compromise with the trade unions was out of the question. The democratic labor movement, a potential opposition in a totalitarian state, had to be destroyed. Accordingly, the day after "National Labor Day," Union leaders Leipart, Grassmann, Wissell, and numerous others were arrested by the Nazis, and on May 13 all union property was confiscated. The Christian and liberal trade union organizations also were subsequently suppressed. A new Nazi Labor Front was created which remained in power until Germany's defeat in World War II.

A fundamental question must be posed. Why did eminent labor leaders, holding socialist convictions in the 'twenties, attempt to compromise with the Nazis during the initial months of the Hitler era? Several factors may have had a bearing on the course of action chosen by these men. The Depression demoralized the labor movement both physically and psychologically. The faith in socialism of some leaders gradually receded and was being replaced by a stress on nationalism, which could have led to an ideological capitulation to the Nazis. Moreover, the leaders expected the Nazis to spare their movement, painfully nurtured through bitter struggles, from the totalitarian web. But they failed to foresee the ruthlessness of the new policy, its drive toward total elimination of the democratic institutions, and its opposition to any non-fascist ideologies. The labor officials were not the only ones, however, to have lacked this vision. The burden of guilt must be placed on most leaders of the democratic groups, since few had the courage to oppose actively the National Socialists at the critical hour.

It was not always so. During most of the Weimar era, the Union, in cooperation with the Social Democratic Party, was able to wield considerable power within the state machinery. It served as a potent weapon for the protection of the Republic against internal and external onslaughts. Only when the fragile democratic structure began to decay from within, did the Union, as a major national institution, gradually lose its power to act. When the crisis came, neither the democratic régime nor the free labor movement had the strength of will to cooperate any more in halting the plunge into the abyss. In this failure to act lay the tragedy of Germany.

A RESULT OF MILITARISM, NOT ECONOMICS?

While German labor in 1932 had lost its militancy, Nazism throve upon and cultivated a brutality, discipline, ruthlessness, and hierarchical concept of social status which many observers believe was rooted in German "militarism." In the first reading below, Professor J. J. Schokking of the University of Cologne points to the foundation provided for Nazism by the militaristic spirit in German society before Hitler. Professor Robert G. L. Waite of Williams College, in the second reading of this section, shows how the First World War intensified this militaristic spirit and how the freebooter units (*Freikorps*) of the postwar period bridged the gap between the war and the rise of the Nazi movement. In the third reading of this section, Gordon A. Craig examines in some detail the specific contributions of army leaders to Hitler's success in the crisis months of 1932–1933. Craig is professor of history at Princeton University and the author of several important studies in German and diplomatic history.

Militarism in German Society

J. J. SCHOKKING

ON WHAT incentives did the Nazis act? From what sources did their will to power originate? Where did the energy by which the machine of their instrumentality was kept in continuous motion come from?

No answer can be given to these questions unless an attempt has been made to see the social significance of militarism in general, and of the militarist tendencies in Germany after the defeat of the Wilhelmian armies in particular.

Where militarism reigns, two attitudes are predominant. The army considers itself, and is treated by the rest of the nation, as a "community" in and of itself, solely integrated by man-to-man contacts of its own makings, and not as an organisational set-up providing an effective collaboration of armed citizens for the national purpose of security. Secondly, the very existence of the socio-political order is assumed to depend on the strength of this self-contained force, not to be merely shielded by it.

Under a system of standing armies militarism has other implications than under a system of conscription.

The professional soldiers of standing armies in non-democratic states are indifferent to the political community. They only know their allegiance to the man who personifies their own "community" — their supreme commander. Beyond that they do not go. As their community consciousness is narrowed down to the confines of the army, there is nothing which induces them to be concerned with the motives of their chief whenever he is acting in his capacity

From Maurice Baumont, John H. E. Fried, Edmond Vermeil, and others, *The Third Reich* (New York, 1955), pp. 482–487. Reprinted by permission of Frederick A. Praeger, Inc.

as political leader, or to concern themselves with the interests of the political community — that is, the nation as a whole. That the army is not only a fighting machine, but possesses also the quality of being valued in its own right as a constitutive element of the socio-political order, is the supreme commander's affair, not theirs.

Now, conscription changes these relationships fundamentally. At the origin of conscription stands Rousseau's democratic view, that to serve as a soldier is every citizen's duty, but that no citizen ought to take up this service as a profession. Nevertheless conscription may be applied as a method of recruitment in states which otherwise remain as militarist as they were before. Under such conditions conscription tends to make participation in the army the exclusive form of community participation, not merely for professional soldiers, but for all men who by the dispositions of the conscription laws are compelled to serve with the colours. The barracks will often enough get the meaning of a home for the conscript soldier, the regiment will be his family, the army emblems his religious symbols, the army regulations the overriding rules of human conduct. On the other hand the army becomes susceptible of losing its special feature of forming a separate "community."

Moreover, though militarism continues to determine the character of political and social life, the introduction of conscription will certainly transform the substance of the state. The army's unique position in the state is no longer taken for granted. After being conscripted into the service, the sons of the people will not follow in a docile fashion the tradition established by the standing armies of the militarist type. They will not be inclined to acknowledge that the supreme commander, on the sole ground of being their warlord, is entitled to dispose of their lives. Yet, as long as militarism continues to shape the socio-political order, they are prevented from exercising the democratic notion according to which the supreme commander is not

more than an outstanding expert, charged by the community of all citizens — i.e., the nation — with the responsibility for defence. There is only one way out of this dilemma. It is feasible that the political institutions and the link-up between military and political leadership be so framed as to make the supreme commander the embodiment of the nation. He would then become the absolute head not only, as he has hitherto been, of the army and the Government, but also of the nation — a kind of military, political, and social autocrat, whose decisions determine how the nation will be structured and what ends it should aspire to attain — in short, a man without whom there would be no nation at all.

Obviously a transformation of this kind involves the people at large. It cannot be brought about unless all layers of society absorb militarism and are ready to think in militarist terms. This means that they have to be imbued with the idea that war is the inevitable destiny of mankind, that victory in war alone gives the fittest a chance to survive, and that the waging of war is man's most natural occupation. The people who want to constitute themselves as a nation must envisage the army as the nation's core and the supreme commander as the incarnation of its collective will.

Germany has passed through all these stages of militarism. Eighteenth-century Prussia exemplified in the most perfect way the militarist state based upon a standing army. The army came first; but as far as Prussia's domestic affairs were concerned, her rulers were always careful to heed the wants of the population and the regulations of the law, and in foreign relations they had an eye for diplomatic no less than for military exigencies. If the prince himself was not an enlightened ruler — as happened, e.g., in the case of Frederick II — a dutiful, law-abiding, and capable bureaucracy were unfalteringly ready to keep the army within its limits. They were, of course, aware of the army's essential significance in politics. However, this was not the soldiers' business, certainly not directly. For them, their concern had to be limited to the army, their task being a restricted one: the army has to fight, or to be prepared to fight. Intent on maintaining the army's so-called "non-political" character, the generals would never be inclined to ignore the outspoken wishes of the bureaucracy. At the same time, generals and bureaucrats were both commanded by the prince, the supreme commander and chief of state.

This Prussian type of militarism became a tradition, deeply rooted in and affecting all social relationships. With the introduction of conscription, new forces were released that were incompatible with it; yet the tradition was not at first weakened. During the greater part of the nineteenth century it continued to shape policies and attitudes. Even in a later period, and up to World War II, it remained quite strong.

It began to lose its impact when, prior to World War I, the military legislation of the Wilhelmian era extended the size of the imperial armed forces at an ever-increasing pace. Then the significance of the combination of militarism with conscription revealed itself fully.

It became apparent that it was necessary to "generalise" militarism — that is, to extend it ever farther. The "old" Prussian militarism was no more than a maxim of statecraft; it was therefore not capable of being spread among the broad masses of the people. In order to inculcate militarism into the popular mind it had to be metamorphosed into a general and all-pervading attitude towards life, towards history, and towards contemporary socio-political conditions. In short, it had to be made into an "ideology."

When propaganda for militarism as an ideology began to be set into motion, by no means all responsible Germans were happy about this development. Even those who took an active part in it sometimes felt ill at ease. They were not always blind to the contradictions between the Prussian

tradition and Kantian ethics in which they had been reared, and their new actions. Nor did it wholly escape them that they were supporting a pseudo-democracy, and thereby raising appetites which one day might lead to demands for a genuine democracy, a system they abhorred.

All this, however, did not prevent them from using every means of psychological conditioning at their disposal. The misgivings they felt when doing so explain at least partly the strange mixture of rigidity and puffed-up enthusiasm which, under the influence of their forced efforts to propagate militarism as an ideology, became more and more one of the most striking features of German social life.

Special emphasis was laid on education by the new militarism. In the face of strong opposition, indoctrination in militarism was gradually made a foremost objective of teaching in German schools and universities.

The question may now be asked: did the attempts to imprint the militarist ideology on the whole of the German people really succeed? Was this people made thoroughly familiar with the idea that nationhood was a matter dependent in all its aspects on the will of the emperor as war-lord, head of the state, and embodiment of the nation in arms? This is often contended, though the arguments which are usually invoked in support of this view are not convincing. Wilhelmian Germany was a highly complicated country, the battlefield of many tendencies. This much may be said. The deliberate effort to impart militarist sentiments to the German people and to marry the Prussian tradition with a popular militarist ideology produced three characteristic features, each of profound significance. The army retained its character of a closed and exclusive community, and consequently, more than in democratic countries, moulded the personalities of the boys who were enlisted. Secondly, the ties which joined the army to the socio-political order remained; in fact, the two became even more strongly allied in the minds of the soldiers and people than they were before. Democracy could therefore not be established in Wilhelmian Germany without both defeat in war and revolution from within. Thirdly, in the event of defeat innumerable young men were in danger of losing their sole community attachments, while state and society would lose their cohesion.

Such was the picture of the situation at the end of World War I. Defeat was not envisaged. But the unexpected happened indeed. After a strenuous war, which in its first stages had raised popular militarism to a high pitch of intensity, defeat came.

With the fall of the army in 1918, the whole structure of Wilhelmian Germany broke asunder. There was no alternative to replace it — at least not immediately. The mere act of founding the Republic — a rather external, a purely constitutional change — was not enough. In order to establish a stable democracy Germany would have had to be reorganised from top to bottom. It required a new social integration, on the basis of democratic principles and usages. The remnants of the Prussian tradition, as well as the effects of the queer, ambivalent propaganda for popular militarism, which had supplemented this tradition in the preceding decades, had to be wiped out. Intentions to do so were not absent, nor was there a lack of men who had the will and the capacity to reframe Germany along democratic lines. In order to succeed, however, they needed freedom from foreign pressures, the immediate prospect of economic recovery and of increasing prosperity, and, most of all, they needed time. None of these conditions was granted to them.

One of the most pernicious effects of the sudden collapse of Germany was that all groups and individuals for whom militarism had become the guiding ideology and the only possible way of life, felt themselves deprived of their beliefs, their community, their nation. They rejected the Re-

public, not so much because they were against the replacement of monarchical institutions by republican ones, as because it represented in their eyes a society which was strange to them and in which they could have no share — a victory of forces which had thrown them back on their own mental and material resources, to manage as best as they could as scattered and isolated individuals. In the great majority of cases these resources were very small or did not exist at all.

Now that the social fabric which had satisfied their wants of sociability had fallen to pieces, many ex-officers and soldiers, hoping to escape the loneliness they were unable to face and somehow to gain a substitute for the lost footholds in life, and also thereby to find an occupation and material support, sought refuge in the several Free Corps, which at the end of the war and in the first post-war years were formed all over Germany. These were fighting units, operating haphazardly under self-appointed leaders. Marching against the Reds in Germany and on Germany's eastern border, resisting the Poles, stimulating local revolts in the Ruhr and elsewhere, they were inspired by the social and political aspirations of the past that had disappeared, and were ever animated by an outright hostility towards the Republic. Otherwise they followed the precepts of their militarist training, which somehow forbade soldiers to intervene constructively in politics or to pursue a positive policy of their own. The inner contradiction of this mental situation was a cause of utter frustration. Despite their tenacity, audacity, and ruthlessness, the Free Corps came to nothing.

National-Socialism was a different movement from the outset. Though born of the same deceptions and urges which led to the creation of the Free Corps, National-Socialism chose another approach.

It did not confine its appeal to demobilised officers and soldiers, but extended it to all militaristically-minded Germans, whatever they were or had been. In the course of time, after the Free Corps had disbanded, many of their former members were to become Nazism's fiercest enemies, while others took the opposite course and found a lasting home under the Nazi roof. In any case among the high echelons of the Nazi hierarchy the proportion of Free Corps veterans was gradually to become very numerous. From their side, however, the Nazis undertook nothing to continue the Free Corps tradition of segregation, but consistently tried to penetrate into all sections of German society.

Moreover, Nazism understood that under the changed conditions a revival of militarism could not be brought about by copying the Wilhelmian methods. It sensed that the spell of the Prussian tradition had to be broken and that a new, more radical, and more exclusively popular orientation was wanted. Nazism realised that the militarism prevalent before World War I had been closely connected with the social and political texture of Imperial Germany. Being aware of the fact that this had been destroyed beyond repair, Nazism foresaw the possibilities of socialising militarism and of creating a powerful nation-in-arms, an armed society, a people living by war and for war. As slogans these notions had already been used by militarist propaganda under the Kaiser, but the will to accept the full consequences of them was absent then. Such a will implied the necessity of throwing overboard all technical inhibitions, all endeavours to direct the socio-political institutions in consonance with the dictates of justice and rationality, and indeed all other doctrines and theories. Instead, the demands of expediency, resulting from total mobilisation for total war, had alone to prevail.

To National-Socialism politics meant the struggle for "naked power" by all means promising rapid success.

The Nazis viewed themselves as the nucleus of the militarised people in the process of becoming, as the military "counter-society" that had one day to take the place of the Weimar Republic and of all other states in which Germans lived. They thought that they had only to increase their numbers and strength in order to reach their political aims. The movement was instrumental to the new German militarism and its quest for power. That in this development the Weimar Republic had to disappear was taken for granted. To reach their ends, however, it was not necessary, in the first instance, to fight it with physical means. For the Nazis a private army had its advantages; it was in a way indispensable, but it could be really effective only if the movement gave priority to the political aim and in pursuit of that knew how to profit from the opportunities which were offered by the Weimar democracy. In contradistinction to the Free Corps, the Nazis discovered that democracy could be wrecked by constant abuse of its liberties. By instinct, rather than by calculation, they knew that once militarist tendencies were developed to the utmost in German society their movement would automatically sweep away the Weimar Republic, and eventually the other European States within whose frontiers Germans were living. . .

The Free Corps: Vanguard of Nazism

ROBERT G. L. WAITE

REVOLUTIONARY Berlin gave birth to a phenomenon absolutely unique in the annals of Prussian military history. Here, in the early days of December 1918 was born a troop of men of battalion strength who were commanded by a noncommissioned officer. When the Second Guard Regiment returned from the Western front they were insulted by the solicitations of the Soldiers' Councils. A group of the regiment's soldiers appealed to their sergeant-major to organize them into a Free Corps. Sergeant-Major Suppe called an organizational meeting at the Zirkus Busch, and founded the Suppe Free Corps. His brigade of some 1,500 men was divided into companies, each of which was commanded by a sergeant. After the Schloss and Marstall fiasco, Suppe joined the Reinhard Brigade, but kept command of his own battalion.

About this time in Kiel, Admiral Loewenfeld founded his Third Naval Brigade as a companion to Ehrhardt's more famous Second Brigade. Like Ehrhardt's Free Corps, the Third Brigade also consisted predominantly of officers, naval cadets, and seasoned petty officers. According to one of its members, each of the company commanders had been a former U-boat commander and all of them wore the coveted *Pour le mérite*, Germany's highest military award. Its "Storm Battalion" was led by Arnauld de la Pierre, the famous submarine hero who had sunk 550,000 tons with his own ship. Loewenfeld writes proudly of his Corps:

[It became] . . . on the whole the strongest Free Corps in Germany, not only in numbers — about 8,000 men — but also in its articula-

tion of infantry, pioneers, artillery (of four calibers), trench mortars, flame-throwers, armored vehicles, tanks, aircraft, and trucks. We could handle every demand of war.

Meanwhile, from Düsseldorf to Königsberg; from Hamburg to Munich, similar groups were forming everywhere. And Noske, from his office in the girls' dormitory, encouraged them all and launched a drive for more troops. Separate recruiting offices were established throughout the Reich and provocative advertisements appeared on billboards and in newspapers:

VOLUNTEERS!
From the West — March to the East!
FLAME–THROWER PERSONNEL
Enlist in the Flame-thrower section of
THE LUETTWITZ CORPS
Immediate pay plus 5 marks daily bonus.
Free food and equipment.

COMRADES
The Spartacist danger has not yet been removed. The Poles press ever farther onto German soil. Can you look on these things with calm?
NO!
Think what your dead comrades would think!
Soldiers, Arise! Prevent Germany from becoming the laughing stock of the earth.
Enroll NOW in
THE HUELSEN FREE CORPS
Recruiting offices:
Bauer Cafe, Unter den Linden,
Potsdam Beer Gardens . . . [etc.]

VOLUNTEERS, FALL OUT!
Patriotic Germans, join the fierce and foolhardy
LUTZOW FREE CORPS.

From Robert G. L. Waite, *Vanguard of Nazism: The Free Corps Movement in Postwar Germany, 1918–1923* (Cambridge, Mass., 1952), pp. 37–44 and 281. Reprinted by permission of the Harvard University Press.

Measured in terms of sheer quantity, the recruiting campaign was immensely successful. By the summer of 1919, thousands of Germans had entered one or another of the volunteer formations. It is extraordinarily difficult to give even a very loose approximation of the size of the movement. Contemporary sources are in flat disagreement. The Independent Socialist, Hugo Haase, in a speech to the National Assembly, pointed with alarm at an illegal army of over a million men. Noske estimates the number at 400,000. Ernst von Salomon has difficulty making up his mind. In one place he says "between 50,000 and 70,000"; in another, "150,000." In part, the difficulty arises from the fact that a "Volunteer" may be defined in a variety of different ways. All the postwar military and semi-military formations were recruited on a volunteer basis. These formations included not only the Free Corps (*Freikorps*) as such, but Emergency Volunteers (*Zeitfreiwilligen*), Civil Guards (*Einwohnerwehr*), and Security Police (*Sicherheitspolizei*), as well as a host of armed student formations such as the *Münster Akademische Wehr*. What further complicates matters is that these latter types sometimes served as local civilian guards and sometimes conducted regular military campaigns along with the Free Corps. Even if we accept the rule-of-thumb criterion suggested by von Salomon and confine ourselves to the "real" Free Corps, that is, only to "those troops capable of coping with any military problem," there is still no agreement. Schmidt-Pauli in the foreword to his history of the movement complains about the difficulty of discussing "over two hundred well organized Free Corps"; while von Salomon insists that the number of such formations never exceeded eighty-five.

Let us estimate, then, that the number of men directly involved in the movement was somewhere between 200,000 and 400,000. The numbers — imprecise as they admittedly are — are nevertheless important. These men practiced a doctrine which differed in no essential way from that political and social cannibalism which was to call itself National Socialism. It is worth remembering that by the summer of 1919 the Free Corps may well have been the most important single power in Germany.

In 1919, the contrast between the strength of the Free Corps and the weakness of Adolf Hitler's movement is glaring. While the Volunteers were sweeping the country with their gospel of race and power, what was Hitler doing? One afternoon during that same summer an obscure political agitator raised his strangely compelling voice to demand that the struggling, newly formed, little German Workers' party purchase three rubber stamps in order to improve its office equipment.

REASONS FOR ENTERING THE FREE CORPS

In addition to general appeals to patriotism, the recruitment campaign emphasized the very real material advantages offered by the Free Corps. Conditions varied in each Corps, but a hypothetical average Volunteer could expect to receive a daily base pay of from 30 to 50 marks; he was guaranteed 200 grams of meat and 75 grams of butter a day; service in the Free Corps counted toward workers' and farmers' pensions; his family received the regular family allotment; at the end of his period of enlistment, the Volunteer drew the pay allotted to all demobilized soldiers; he was, of course, completely clothed at government expense. Officers received extra bonuses which varied with the area in which they served. The Volunteers were satisfied with the arrangements. One of them writes: "Noske added 5 marks [to the regular pay], and the Bavarian government another 5. Then too, we got plenty of beer and cigarettes and a quarter of a liter of wine a day. We had a good time."

Why, then, did they join the Free Corps? Because as patriots they wanted to save the Fatherland from internal anarchy and the threat of invasion? Because of assurance of material well-being? These, indubitably, were factors. But they only supply a part — not a very important part —

of the answer. There was a better reason for entering the movement. It was that the Free Corps gave high promise of solving the basic psychological and social problems which confronted this generation which was indeed "the Generation of the Uprooted and Disinherited." It is not possible to understand the appeal of the volunteers without first understanding the tremendous psychological repercussions which the defeat of 1918 had on the German mind. It left a generation of men bewildered, embittered, and filled with a terrible hatred against the world which had betrayed them. Let us look more closely at the motivations of the two groups which together formed the great majority of all Volunteers: the front soldiers and the student youth of Germany.

The type of veteran discussed in the previous chapter returned from the War with roots which could not find nourishment in the soil of a *bürgerlich* society. He saw in the new Republic a feeble government of pacifists which had betrayed the Army. Such a society could neither appreciate nor understand him; consequently, after the first weariness of the front had passed, he joined the Free Corps. Here he found comradeship, understanding, economic security, and a continuation of the military life he had learned to love. Friedrich Wilhelm Heinz, a War volunteer at sixteen, member of the Ehrhardt Brigade, and subsequently supreme S.A. Leader for Western Germany, is representative of the men who could never demobilize psychologically:

People told us that the War was over. That made us laugh. We ourselves are the War. Its flame burns strongly in us. It envelops our whole being and fascinates us with the enticing urge to destroy. We obeyed . . . and marched onto the battlefields of the postwar World just as we had gone into battle on the Western Front: singing, reckless and filled with the joy of adventure as we marched to the attack; silent, deadly, remorseless in battle.

The Free Corps leader who was to become Minister President of Saxony under Hitler tells us that this "pure freebooter type" was the most common of all Volunteers, and the type most sought after by the *Freikorpsführer*:

The pure *Landsknechte* didn't much care why or for whom they fought. The main thing for them was that they *were* fighting . . . War had become their career. They had no desire to look for another . . . War made them happy — what more can you ask? I liked this group . . . such freebooters were useful to our purposes in every respect.

Next to the war veterans, students formed the largest group in the Free Corps. For the most part, they were young idealists who had been brought up to believe in the moral righteousness of Germany's cause. They were stunned by the magnitude and the suddenness of the collapse. They demanded immediate and drastic action to save the Fatherland. This was no time for moderation, for the half-measures proposed by those bungling politicians in Weimar. An astute observer of his generation has caught the attitude perfectly in one phrase: "Radicalism is trumps." Some of them entered politics with results that are succinctly described by Dr. Edgar J. Jung in an often-quoted article entitled, "The Tragedy of the War Generation":

One after the other of them, in danger of starvation . . . resignedly bowed under the yoke of a period whose catch word was peace and money-grabbing. . . . But others would not give in to so hard a fate. Clumsily ignorant but intransigent . . . they entered domestic politics with the courage of despair. . . . They drew up programs without knowledge, enthused over actions without forces, and concocted projects without reality.

And many of them enlisted in the Volunteers. During the War, they had identified themselves with the front soldier; and now they felt the impact of the defeat as keenly as did their heroes. The accident of age and what they felt was a traitorous armistice had cheated them of their right to fight for the Fatherland and to participate in the glories and the romance of battle. The Free Corps gave them another chance. And above all, like the National Socialism which was in a real sense its heir, the Free Corps movement answered the pressing psychological need of the confused and the insecure. It gave them a chance to forget their own inefficacy by identifying themselves with a movement which promised them everything which they lacked as individuals: the opportunity for dramatic action and power. They welcomed their chance to barter personal freedom for a new security and a new pride in participating in power.

A great deal of the literature of postwar Germany is unreadable, irresponsible bombast. But the writings of Ernst von Salomon are an honest reflection of the chaotic and embittered mind of his generation. As a boy of sixteen, he watched the defeated Army return to Berlin. His reaction is worth quoting at some length, for it was the reaction of thousands of his fellow students:

Their eyes were hidden in the shadow thrown by the peaks of their caps, sunk in dark hollows, grey and sharp. These eyes looked neither to the right nor to the left. They remained fixed before them, as if under the spell of a terrifying goal . . . God! What a look they had, those men! Those thin faces, impassive under their helmets, those bony limbs, those ragged clothes covered with dirt! They advanced step by step and around them grew the void of a great emptiness . . .

But here was their home, here warmth and fellowship awaited them — then why did they not cry out with joy? Why didn't they laugh and shout? . . . Why didn't they even look at us? . . . Oh, God! This was terrible! Somebody had lied to us. These were not our heroes, our defenders of the Homeland! These men did not belong to us at all. Everything we had hoped, thought and said had become terribly wrong . . . What a mistake! What a ghastly mistake! . . . These men had come from a totally different world! . . . Yes, that was it! Suddenly I understood.

These men were not workers, farmers, students . . . These men were soldiers . . . united in the bonds of blood and sacrifice. Their home was the Front — it was for them

Homeland! Fatherland! *Volk!* Nation! That is why, yes, that is why they could never belong to us. That is the reason for this stolid, moving, spectral return . . . War moved them; war dominated them; they could never abandon it; never come home. They would always carry the Front in their blood: the approaching death, the glorious suspense, the suffering, the smoke, the cold steel . . .

And suddenly they were supposed to become peaceful citizens in a *bürgerlich* world! Oh, no! That was a transplanting, a counterfeit which was bound to fail . . . The war is ended but the warriors still march! . . .

Posters hung in the street corners, volunteers were sought. Formations were to be organized to defend our Eastern frontiers. On the day after the entrance of the troops into the city, I volunteered. I was accepted, I was equipped. I too was a soldier.

. . . Throughout this study, it has been necessary to take serious issue with National Socialist interpretation of the nature and importance of the German Free Corps Movement. Nevertheless, the Nazis are right in their chief contention: the Free Corps did make fundamental and direct contributions to Hitler's Germany.

They made a negative contribution of first-rate importance. The Weimar Republic was indeed, as Scheidemann once said in a brilliant metaphor, a candle burning at both ends. The Free Corps and their successor organizations were largely responsible for the fact that the flame at the Right end of the candle burned more brightly and melted more wax than its competitor on the Left.

They made specific positive contributions. In spite of the toll taken by the Blood Purge, hundreds of the Freebooters rose to positions of power in the National Socialist regime. They contributed a well-developed leadership principle, labor camps, youth groups, violent racism, and the mystic adoration of the *Volk* soul.

Yet the real importance of the movement lies in none of these things. It lies in that brutality of spirit and in that exaltation of power which the men of the Free Corps bequeathed to the Third Reich.

The Guilt of the Old Army

GORDON A. CRAIG

I N THE CRITICAL years of the Weimar Republic, as in previous periods of German history, the army played a decisive part in determining the political destiny of the nation. The most dangerous enemies of the republic realized that they could not hope to overthrow it unless they secured at least the sympathetic neutrality of the army; and Hitler for one was guided by that knowledge in all phases of his policy before 1933. Hitler set out deliberately to play upon the dissatisfaction which existed within the army, and while his promises of a restored and expanded military establishment gradually enticed the bulk of the junior officers to his support, his charges that the republican régime lacked national spirit and failed adequately to defend the interests of the state found a sympathetic response in the hearts of the officer corps in general. Thus the fateful political change of 30 January 1933 was supported, at least tacitly, by the army. . . .

The last unhappy phase in the history of the Weimar Republic was one, therefore, in which the army was more continuously and intimately involved in domestic politics than it had been under either Seeckt or Groener. This was made abundantly clear in the negotiations which led to the formation of the Papen government. It was Schleicher who urged Hindenburg to appoint Franz von Papen as Bruening's successor, who first broached the matter to Papen himself, who nominated most of his ministerial colleagues, and who conducted the negotiations which were designed to win Hitler's forbearance as the new cabinet began its work. And in all this, as Papen himself has written, "Schleicher left . . . no doubt that he was acting as spokesman for the army, the only stable organization remaining in the State."

The first fruits of Schleicher's grand design were hardly impressive. Papen's appointment as Chancellor was received with considerable stupefaction by a country which, with reason, had never been able to take the gentleman jockey, and war-time military attaché in the United States, very seriously; and wits were quick to point out that the only qualifications for a ministerial portfolio in the new government seemed to be a background in the *Gardekürassier* Regiment or the title Freiherr (Baron). The initial criticism deepened as the consequences of Schleicher's negotiations with Hitler became apparent. In return for an equivocal promise to support the new government, Hitler had been assured that new elections for the Reichstag would be held and that the decree abolishing the S.A. would be repealed. The Reichstag was consequently dissolved on 4 June and the S.A. *Verbot* rescinded on the 15th. Hitler immediately turned his full attention to the task of scoring new gains in the forthcoming elections, and he loosed his liberated storm troopers against his opponents. A new wave of violence swept over the country, reaching its peak in riots at Altona on 17 July when fifteen persons were killed and fifty injured.

These events, which weakened whatever meagre popular support the new government possessed, did not disturb Schleicher or cause him to deviate from his course. He agreed with his fellow cabinet ministers — for he had undertaken to serve as Reichswehr Minister in Papen's government —

From Gordon A. Craig, *The Politics of the Prussian Army, 1640–1945* (Oxford, 1955), pp. xviii, 455–459, and 461–466. Reprinted by permission of the Clarendon Press.

that it would be expedient to reimpose the ban on political demonstrations and parades, even if this was likely to strain Hitler's "tolerance" to the breaking point. But at the same time, he insisted that the time had come to strike out at the Social Democrats, and in a way designed simultaneously to placate Hitler and to advance the government's plan of centralizing political authority in the country. The main stronghold of Social Democratic power since 1929 had been the Prussian government; and Prussia was currently governed by a Socialist-Centre coalition government, the Braun-Severing government, although this no longer represented a majority in the *Landtag* and was ruling *ad interim*. Schleicher proposed the deposition of the Prussian ministers and their replacement by a Reich Commissioner; and, to justify such high-handed action, he secured from friendly sources within the Prussian Ministry of the Interior what purported to be evidence that the Prussian department of police was under communist influence, that it had been lax in dealing with communist demonstrations and that, consequently, it was responsible for the disorders at Altona and elsewhere.

Papen was in full agreement with the proposed plan. After securing the approval of the President and ordering General Gerd von Rundstedt, commanding *Wehrkreis III*, to alert his troops for immediate action, the Chancellor and the Reichswehr Minister on 20 July informed the flabbergasted Prussian ministers that they were to be replaced by a Reich Commissioner in the person of Papen. The angry officials protested loudly but in vain, and, on the same day, were physically ejected from their offices. Neither on the 20th nor on succeeding days did anything resembling active resistance materialize, for neither the *Reichsbanner* nor the trade unions were, in the opinion of their leaders, strong enough to oppose the government's stroke, and the police could not be counted on to test their strength against that of the local garrisons.

For Papen and Schleicher, however, this well-executed coup was an empty victory. Neither it, nor Papen's success in freeing Germany from reparations at the Lausanne conference, nor even his carefully calculated withdrawal from the Disarmament conference on 23 July served to increase the reputation or the popularity of the government; and this was made unmistakably clear in the national elections of 31 July. When the votes were counted and the Reichstag seats apportioned, it was patent that the Cabinet of Barons had been rejected by an overwhelming majority of the people. The only two parties upon whom Papen could rely with any assurance — the Nationalists and the *Volkspartei* — won only forty-four seats between them. On the other hand, the nazis — whose thunder Schleicher and Papen had hoped to steal by their coup in Prussia — doubled their representation, winning 230 seats and becoming the largest party in the Reichstag. There was now no hope that Hitler would tolerate Papen further. The nazi chief burned for power and, when it was refused him in the now famous interview with Hindenburg on 13 August, he wasted no time in going on the offensive. When Papen met the Reichstag for the first time on 12 September, he was forced to dissolve it immediately, for the nazis and the communists combined to defeat him overwhelmingly in a vote of confidence. This necessitated new elections and, when they were held, in the first week of November, Papen fared little better than he had in July. Ninety per cent of the votes cast were still against the government.

In mid-October Josef Goebbels had written in his diary: "The Reichswehr has already fallen away from the Cabinet. Upon what will it base itself now?" The remark was perceptive, if premature. It was only after the November elections that army support was withdrawn from Papen, and this, of course, was Schleicher's doing. The general had, without doubt, become increasingly displeased with Papen in the weeks since the July coup, for the Chancellor had not only developed an irritating habit of making up his own mind on important issues, but was also in a fair way to supplanting Schleicher in the affections of the President. But it was the November election results which raised more basic differences. The most salient feature of the elections was the sharp setback suffered by the nazis — a loss of two million votes and thirty-four Reichstag seats. To Schleicher this proved that the time had come to put into effect the second part of his programme, the operation designed to split the National Socialist party. He was aware that Gregor Strasser, the leader of that party's powerful political organization, was deeply discouraged by the election returns, and believed that they foreshadowed a precipitous decline in party fortunes. Schleicher thought that Strasser would be willing to join a new government and that he would be supported by important elements of the party, including Roehm. To make this new combination possible, however, Papen would have to step down, for neither Strasser nor Roehm would be prepared to serve under him.

Papen, on the other hand, had developed a love for office which was — despite all the disclaimers which he makes in his memoirs — to persist until 1945. He had no intention of stepping down. He would, he insisted, make a last effort to secure, by negotiation with the parties, a workable parliamentary majority. If this failed, as it almost certainly would, he would summon Hitler and demand that he either demonstrate that he could obtain such a majority or that he enter the cabinet as Vice-Chancellor. If Hitler refused, then all attempts to observe constitutional propriety must be abandoned. The Reichstag — and if necessary the opposition parties, and the trade unions — should be dissolved and the cabinet should rule quite openly by presidential decree backed by the authority of the army.

With the President's backing, the first steps of the Papen programme were taken. The parties were canvassed and emphatically rejected the suggestion that they support the cabinet. For five days, between 19 and 24 November, Hindenburg, his secretary Meissner, and Papen conducted acrimonious negotiations with Hitler, only to receive in the end his flat refusal to accept anything but a grant of full power. After that there was nothing left for Papen but the third alternative — the open violation of the constitution; and in an interview with Hindenburg and Schleicher on 1 December, he proposed this.

The fact that the President, despite his sincere desire to remain true to his constitutional oath, gave his approval to Papen's plan, shows how completely he had fallen under the spell of the *Herrenreiter*. Hindenburg, indeed, proved wholly impervious to all of the rather disingenuous arguments which Schleicher now made in favour of legality, and he was frankly sceptical of the general's claim that he could destroy the nazis without departing from the letter of the constitution. He preferred, he said, to go on with Papen. In consequence, Schleicher was compelled to resort to the same kind of forcing play which had served to get rid of Groener and Bruening. He brought the influence of the army to bear against the Chancellor.

At a meeting of the full cabinet on 2 December Schleicher came out flatly against the Papen proposals. . . .

The Chancellor repaired to Hindenburg who listened in silence to the news. Then the President said: "My dear Papen, you will not think much of me if I change my mind. But I am too old and have been through too much to accept the responsibility for a civil war. Our only hope is to let Schleicher try his luck."

Thus Schleicher himself — rather reluctantly, since he knew that his political talent was best exercised behind the scenes — became Chancellor in the first week of December. A few days later, Goebbels wrote cheerfully in his diary: "A Jew has written a book called 'The Rise of Schleicher,' of which a huge edition is being published. A great pity, since when it appears in the shop windows von Schleicher will have disappeared from the

political stage." Once again the little doctor's gift of prophecy was working well.
Schleicher's chancellorship, which marked
the highest point of army influence in the
history of the republic, was brief and in-
glorious. It was notable, however, in one
respect. Despite its brevity, it was long
enough for Schleicher and the generals
who supported him to execute a remarkable
volte-face. In early December they were
determined that Hitler must not come to
power and confident that they could prevent this. By late January they were determined that he *must* come to power and
frightened lest something should occur to
postpone his doing so.

The failure of Schleicher's chancellorship was made inevitable within a week of
his assumption of office. He had staked
everything on his ability to detach Gregor
Strasser from Hitler's side, and his confidence in his influence over Strasser was, in
fact, justified. He erred, however, in as-
suming that Strasser's defection would
break up the National Socialist party; and,
basically, his mistake arose from his over-
estimation of Strasser's capacities and his
under-estimation of Hitler's political genius
in moments of crisis.

On 3 December Schleicher invited
Strasser to join his cabinet as Vice-Chancellor and Minister-President of Prussia.
For the next five days there were heated
discussions in the inner circles of the nazi
party, with Strasser urging that the offer
must be accepted in order to avoid new
elections which might be disastrous for the
party, and Goering and Goebbels staunchly
opposing this course as being the rankest
kind of defeatism. After momentary hesitation, Hitler vetoed the Strasser policy
and, on 7 December, accused the chief of
the party's political organization of seeking
to replace him as Leader. Strasser hotly
denied the charge and, on the following
day, resigned from the party. But there his
resistance stopped. Far from seeking to
carry all or part of the party with him, as
Schleicher had expected, he washed his

hands of the whole business and took his
family off for a vacation in Italy.

Hitler, on the other hand, in an explo-
sion of that demoniac rage which always
cowed his party comrades when they were
exposed to it, threatened to commit suicide
if the party fell to pieces and then pro-
ceeded to smash the political organization
which Strasser had ruled so long, to set up
a new central party commission under
Rudolf Hess, and to bully the deputies and
gauleiters into new pledges of uncondi-
tional loyalty. By mid-December the party
was unquestionably united behind the
Leader; and that fact spelled failure for
the scheme which Schleicher had elabo-
rated in the cabinet meeting of 2 December.

The Chancellor was forced then to do
what Papen had done before him — to make
the dismal round of the parties, seeking
support which would give him a workable
majority when the Reichstag re-convened.
But here his past record for deviousness
told against him in his negotiations with
the middle and left parties, while the promises he made in order to allay their sus-
picions alienated the parties of the right.
Remembering the *coup* in Prussia, the di-
rectorate of the Social Democratic party not
only rejected Schleicher's initial overtures,
and advised the trade union leadership to
do the same, but was openly scornful when
the Chancellor promised fundamental reforms to relieve unemployment and a
scheme of land settlement to alleviate the
distress of the peasantry. The only tangible
effect, indeed, of the last mentioned plan
was to destroy what support Schleicher had
in conservative circles, for, on 12 January,
the *Landbund* delivered a broadside
against the government, accusing it — as it
had once accused Bruening — of desiring
to impose agrarian bolshevism on the eastern districts of the Reich. The persistence
with which Schleicher clung to his agrarian
policy — and his threat to publish details of
the *Osthilfe* scandals of 1927–8 if the resistance of the *Landbund* did not cease —
not only influenced the decision of the

Nationalist party to withdraw its support from the government — a step announced on 20 January — but sensibly weakened Schleicher's popularity in the army, whose officer corps, after all, was still recruited from the very families which would suffer most from the execution of his projects.

Schleicher ended up then with even less party backing than his predecessor. And, this being so, he was forced to go to the President and make precisely the same request that his predecessor had made on 1 December. On 23 January he told the President that the Reichstag must be dissolved and that Germany must be ruled, under article 48 of the constitution, by what amounted to military dictatorship. Hindenburg was a very old and infirm man who suffered frequent lapses of memory, but he had no difficulty in remembering the arguments which Schleicher had used against this very solution only two months before.

On December 2 [he said] you declared that such a measure would lead to civil war. The Army and the police, in your opinion, were not strong enough to deal with internal unrest on a large scale. Since then the situation has been worsening for seven weeks. The Nazis consider themselves in a stronger position, and the left wing is more radical in its intentions than ever. If civil war was likely then, it is even more so now, and the Army will be still less capable of coping with it. In these circumstances I cannot possibly accede to your request for dissolution of the Reichstag and *carte blanche* to deal with the situation.

The President ordered Schleicher to go on with his search for a majority, and the Chancellor went through the motions of doing so. But Schleicher was well aware that his fall was only a matter of days away, and he felt that the time would be better spent in influencing the choice of a successor. This was, after all, a matter which vitally concerned the army, and Schleicher still claimed to speak for that body.

Practically speaking, there were only two possible successors: Hitler and Papen. Hitler, whose fortunes had seemed to be on the down-grade in January, had been strengthened by the establishment of relations with a group of Rhenish-Westphalian industrialists and bankers who assumed responsibility for the debts of his party and were openly calling for his elevation to power. The ebb-tide of party fortunes seemed to have turned, and in local elections the nazis had registered heavy successes within the past weeks. Hitler's appointment to the chancellorship would have seemed a certainty if it had not been for Hindenburg's past record of opposition to him and the President's deep affection for Papen. There was no doubt that Papen wanted office again; and, in view of Hindenburg's feelings, he had an excellent chance of getting it.

Of the two solutions Schleicher preferred the first. His reasons for this were not entirely rational and certainly by no means free of personal prejudice. But he seems to have calculated — as so many others did — that if Hitler assumed the responsibilities of office he would become more moderate in his views and would be susceptible to management by other agencies, notably by the army. If, on the other hand, Papen became Chancellor, Hitler might well raise the standard of revolt, and the army would be placed in the awkward position of having to defend Papen. The general never doubted that the army would have fought cheerfully against Hitler for a Schleicher cabinet; but he refused to believe that it would do the same for Papen, or that it should be forced to do so.

In the last days of January 1933 Schleicher was desperately anxious lest a new Papen government be formed. On 27 January he asked Hammerstein to use the occasion of General von dem Bussche's customary report to the President on personnel affairs in the officer corps to sound Hindenburg out on his intentions. Hammerstein did so and was severely snubbed for his pains, being told that he would be better advised to spend his time thinking of ways of improving manoeuvres rather than in meddling in political matters. However, the President added, "I have no intention whatever of making that Austrian corporal either Minister of Defence or Chancellor of the Reich." This alarmed Schleicher even farther. On the following day, when he went to the President to tell him that the cabinet was resolved to resign unless the powers requested on the 23rd were granted, he tried to argue that the formation of a new Papen government would be disastrous for Germany. The only response he received was a set speech accepting his resignation.

Until the formation of a new government, of course, Schleicher was still Chancellor and Minister of Defence and, with his friend Hammerstein, had direct command over the army. But on 29 January Schleicher learned that General Werner von Blomberg, commanding *Wehrkreis I* and currently a member of the German delegation to the Disarmament conference, had been ordered by the President to return to Berlin and to report to him personally rather than to the Bendlerstrasse (War Ministry), as custom required. This seemed to denote an intention on Hindenburg's part of removing the army from the control of its present commanders by appointing Blomberg as Minister of Defence, after he had promised army support to Papen. In short, if Schleicher and Hammerstein were to block Papen, they were, they thought, going to have to move fast.

The true measure of their desperation in these last days is shown by the fact that the idea of arresting the President and his entourage was frankly discussed by Schleicher's intimates. More important, at least two plain intimations of this possibility were made to Hitler. On the afternoon of 29 January Hammerstein — the man who Groener had believed would oppose a nazi seizure of power "with brutality" — was dispatched by Schleicher to ask Hitler about the state of his current negotiations with Papen and to tell him that, if he thought that Papen was planning to form a government which would exclude him, the generals would be willing "to influence the position." That same night Werner von Alvensleben, one of Schleicher's close associates, went — again at the general's request — to Goebbels's house where a group of nazi chieftains was anxiously awaiting final confirmation of Hitler's appointment as Chancellor and of the President's willingness to dissolve the Reichstag. Alvensleben took the occasion to say to Hitler: "If the Palace crowd are only playing with you, the Reichswehr Minister and the Chief of the *Heeresleitung* will have to turn out the Potsdam garrison and clean out the whole pig-sty from the Wilhelmstrasse."

These were astonishing *démarches,* so astonishing, indeed, that Hitler does not seem to have known what construction to place upon them and secretly took precautions to guard against an army *Putsch,* which might be directed against himself. The Fuehrer's suspicion, while understandable, was unjustified. At this crucial moment in German history, the army command had swung to his side. The only *Putsch* which Schleicher and Hammerstein now contemplated was one which would make certain his appointment. Such action was not, it is true, necessary; and Hitler became Chancellor on 30 January without the intervention of the Potsdam garrisons. But surely the will was as important here as the deed would have been; and Hitler himself later admitted that "if . . . the Army had not stood on our side, then we should not be standing here today.". . .

THE NEMESIS OF WESTERN MASS DEMOCRACY

The author of both the readings in this section vigorously rejects the interpretation set forth above by Craig. Gerhard Ritter contends that the Nazi victory was not due to the support of the German army leaders but of the German masses, who saw in Hitler "a man of the people" and put him into power through the operations of the democratic system. Ritter, distinguished professor at Freiburg-im-Breisgau, has written many books about medieval and modern German history. Among his more recent volumes are: *Europa und die deutsche Frage* . . . (Munich, 1947); *Staatskunst und Kriegshandwerk*, Vol. I (Munich, 1954), Vol. II in preparation; and *Carl Goerdeler und die deutsche Widerstandsbewegung* (Stuttgart, 1955).

The Army Not Guilty

GERHARD RITTER

THE QUESTION regarding the relationship between the military and politics in Germany is one which can be answered by examining the nature of German "militarism." There is no other topic which stirs public opinion in Germany as much as this one. And why not? After all, Adolf Hitler's state was nothing but an attempt to militarize the entire German nation. During his time, soldierly conduct, preparedness, eagerness to serve and a martial mind were considered the highest of all political and social virtues. Then came the destruction of Germany by allied air-raids and the collapse in 1945 followed by three terrible years of want and hunger. A veritable deluge of allied anti-militaristic propaganda flooded Germany. The public prosecutors of the Nuremberg Trials accused the entire German general staff of being a criminal organization for destroying world peace. This general indictment was refused, but numerous high-ranking military leaders had to go to presumptive arrest and most generals had to endure a long period of war captivity which they considered humiliating. On top of this the German public was aroused to great excitement by what became known of the so-called Landsberg Trials.

These very energetic efforts by the Allies to "re-educate" the militaristically educated German nation towards a fundamental pacifism have not remained without far-reaching consequences. That which had, since the War of Liberation against Napoleon I, one hundred and fifty years ago, become the greatest pride of every patriot,

From Gerhard Ritter, "The Military and Politics in Germany," *Journal of Central European Affairs*, XVII (October, 1957), 259–260, 265, and 268–270. Reprinted by permission of S. H. Thomson and Gerhard Ritter.

namely, to defend the fatherland with weapon in hand, had suddenly acquired a stigma. The martial mind and readiness to serve state and nation were suspected of being forms of rowdyism. Military discipline was pilloried and ridiculed as "blind obedience" and slandered as lack of individual courage. The lack of freedom-mindedness was called a basic vice of the German people. Considerable sections of the German people, especially of the younger generation and the working classes, were eager to accept these new teachings. Their effectiveness was increased by a religious pacifism being preached in the churches, especially those of the Protestant faiths. They gained many adherents. Doubtless the one factor that is working most strongly against the German people's readiness to serve is the fact that at the end of the war, after untold miseries and sacrifices, the German soldier was not released to go home immediately after the end of fighting, but was at first kept in labor camps abroad, in many cases — especially in Russia — for long years, where he was sentenced to forced labor, just like a war criminal, apparently for having done his duty as a soldier. The horrors of the Russian prisoner-of-war camps are the strongest possible propaganda against war and against being a soldier. There is no way of telling how all these experiences will hamper the attempt suddenly to build up a new German army. For the time being I am under the disquieting impression that those who today voluntarily resolve to put on a uniform again and to take upon themselves the hard duties of a soldier find that the German people meet them with so little sympathy and with so much distrust and dislike — even open hatred — that especially persons of the greatest moral value are being deterred.

The question about the nature of the so-called German "militarism" has always had an importance for German internal politics that can hardly be overestimated. It is imperative to see without bias the positive achievements of the German profession of arms as well as its dangers and shortcomings, and to distinguish clearly between being a soldier and "militarism," which are not at all identical. It is equally urgent to correct certain wrong ideas which for a long time have enjoyed popularity abroad about the German military and its influence on German politics and society. I can imagine that especially for an American it will be hard to understand correctly this aspect of German life, since all the historical conditions of Germany differ widely from those across the ocean. There can hardly be a greater contrast of international political conditions than there is between the United States and Germany. Up to World War I the United States lived very remote from the struggles for power being fought on the old European continent. From the military point of view it was practically unassailable from without owing to its separation from other countries by water. It was known that Thomas Jefferson had believed and hoped the United States would always pursue a policy of peace without employing military might. Thus, in America the army has, up to the beginning of this century, played an active rôle only in rare and exceptional cases, and fostering a martial spirit was not necessary in the young American nation. How totally different, however, was the situation of Germany, and above all of Prussia, in the middle of Europe! Without continuous effort and without strong military armament Prussia and Germany would never have been able to gain and maintain independence and freedom. Being without protection by natural boundaries in the East and West, it always faced the danger of being conquered from without and becoming the battleground of the great continental powers. That explains why in Germany the army, the profession of arms, occupied a much more central position in life than in England and the United States. . . .

Looking back on the past 100 years we notice that the War of Liberation of 1813–15, as well as the wars of 1866 and 1870–71, brought about great and lasting success relatively quickly, achieving it without extremely heavy sacrifices. It is natural that to us Germans war appeared in a somewhat idealistic light, a physical, spiritual and moral test of the people. Its destruction of culture was considered secondary. The universal conscription (without proxy), since 1867 extended over all of Germany, gradually funneling the entire growing generation through the army, resulted in a rapidly increasing influence of military thinking on wide strata of the population. It became the ambition of the educated youth, as reserve officers, to adapt themselves to the social customs of the active officer corps in which the nobility was still predominant. The younger generation carried a great deal of these customs over into civilian life, and soon national occasions were unthinkable without military parades. The notions "smart" or "soft," originating from military drill on the drill field, were also used to judge political conditions, especially when criticizing the official foreign policy of the Reich. The ideal of "standing smartly," of "resolute behavior" and of "plucky tone" did a great deal to confuse the political ideas of the German citizenry. Wherever "standing smartly" and "resolute behavior" showed through the daily life and in the behavior of the individual German, they naturally made the German disliked abroad and gave him the reputation of being a hard-to-bear "militarist." In fact, if "militarism" is to signify that military thinking and military behavior play too great a part in a nation's life, it cannot be denied that throughout the last decades of the Bismarck state there was a German militarism and that, in its effect upon politics, it was not harmless.

It is a totally different question whether the official course of German foreign policy also was ruled by too great a military preparedness or even by direct influences from the army. It is not easy to answer in a few words. . . .

Taken together the generals' attitude during the Third Reich showed very clearly that these soldiers had also learned from the experiences of the First World War and were aware that Germany's powers would never be sufficient to fight a Second World War – not even should an ultra-modern armament secure her initial superiority over her neighbors. The concept that the German generals of 1939 were just like the militaristic "Supreme Army Command" of 1914–18, which was the case especially in England, had truly fateful results during the Second World War, one of them being the completely wrong judgment of the military opposition to Hitler.

The rapid rise to power of the National-Socialist Party after 1931 cannot be explained by any political activity of the military. To be sure many officers sympathized with Hitler because he promised them a quick and strong rearmament. But there also were decided enemies of his proletarian, noisy, people's movement, especially among the highest leaders. In January of 1933, the Commander-in-Chief, Baronet von Hammerstein, formally protested to the Reich President against the selection of Hitler as Schleicher's successor, saying it would be "intolerable" for the Reichswehr. There is no doubt that the Weimar Republic was not "steamrollered" by army "militarists," but rather by the militarists of a nationalistic people's movement. And yet it will be impossible immediately and without discrimination to denounce as militarists all of these civilian followers of Hitler. The great majority of those hailing the dangerous demagogue did not expect from him a new war but something quite different: a bridging of the previously described deep gap that divided the nation – the gap between left and right, between the followers of nationalist fight slogans and the socialist advocates of welfare and reconciliation – a new unity in a community of the people, the "National Socialists," forming an arch over all the parties. Out of the inner regeneration of the German people thus to take place there was to result, all by itself and without a new war, a tremendous increase of German power and of German prestige in the world. All that would soon be achieved by breaking the "shackles of Versailles." Thus Hitler preached, and that was the hope of the mass of people who voted for him.

In fact, as is only too well known, no expectation has ever been more cruelly disappointed. For our topic the figure of Hitler is interesting above all since it shows more clearly than the others how little the outer organization of state leadership means in comparison to the spirit which imbues the leading men. Organizational means can never solve the problem at hand. Never has the army been more dependent upon the political state leadership than was the case under Hitler. Never has the organizational unity of the leadership of the armed forces, as well as the predominance of the political leader over the soldier, been as perfectly assured as under him. Had he been a genuine statesman, there never would have been so splendid a chance as there was under his leadership, really to overcome the dangers of militarism and to employ so massive a fighting force to safeguard European peace, and for a healthy and lasting order on our continent. Instead, in the event the General Staff vainly tried before as well as during the war to bring an element of moderation into politics (reversing a well-known quotation of Clausewitz') basing their position on military-technical arguments! Thus the natural relationship between the political leaders and the military was in fact completely reversed. . . .

Everything that came later, the total mobilization and militarization of our people by Hitler, did not originate with the generals, just as the Second World War did not, but rather from a political people's movement. To be sure, Hitler was able to find support in the martial instincts and the basic preparedness of the German people. However, he misused them badly against the particular protests of the generals. If I may dare suggest a practical solution from all these historical experiences it will be that building a new German army need not necessarily push our political leadership on a militaristic track and make it dependent on the militaristic direction of any generals. Even the Weimar Republic on the whole successfully kept the army its obedient tool; neither Kapp's coup of 1920 nor Schleicher's policy of 1932 may be interpreted as actions of the army. And yet the army, led by von Seeckt and other former imperial officers, was facing the Republican government with more than cool reserve — basically even with an extremely strong inner aversion. . . .

The Fault of Mass Democracy

GERHARD RITTER

THE WEIMAR Republic failed because it did not succeed in winning general confidence, in becoming genuinely popular through successes which could be appreciated from a distance. So the rejection of Democratic slogans became one of the essential conditions for the rise of Hitler's Party. But to attribute this rejection simply to "the Germans' lack of a sense of liberty" explains nothing; it only disguises

From Maurice Baumont, John H. E. Fried, Edmond Vermeil, and others, *The Third Reich* (New York, 1955), pp. 389–395, 396–397, 399–400, 402–403, and 410–412. Reprinted by permission of Frederick A. Praeger, Inc.

with a grand phrase the true historical problem: the reasons why the chances of liberals have much diminished in this century, particularly in Germany after the First World War.

The desire to replace the unsettled parliamentary coalition governments with a strong and lasting authority certainly played a very large part in Hitler's rise to power. In his propaganda for such an authority Hitler never ceased to praise, as an ideal model for the constitution of the state, the army, with its definite orders and clear responsibility derived from above, not from below, from those who lead, and not from those who are led; and this won the approval of many old soldiers of the First World War, just as Mussolini did when with his Blackshirts he appealed to the instincts of the old "front-line soldiers" and "fighting men." These instincts were certainly much more developed in Germany than in Italy. Perhaps, too, the pedantic eagerness to serve with which the subalterns carried out their *Führer's* orders and plans after the establishment of the dictatorship was greater in Germany.

The great electoral successes of Hitler since 1930, however, cannot be explained by the Germans' wish to find in political life a military discipline, by a desire to be given orders and to be able to obey them. The masses who rallied to him did not at all believe that they were helping a dictator to seize power; they supported a man of the people who had their confidence and from whom they expected the fulfillment of their wishes — of a thousand vast hopes.

The same thing had already occurred in Italy, and its repetition after so few years is a striking proof of the fact that ordinary men never learn anything from history. Hitler had clearly copied from Mussolini the technique of setting up, without a *coup d'état* as such and without violating the constitution, a one party state.

In any case, the German dictatorship was not the first, but the last to be established in Europe, and it became by far the most dangerous (if the Russian Bolshevist dictatorship is ignored).

The conclusion is, therefore, that in order to examine the historical foundations of National-Socialism, one must first of all see what it was in twentieth-century Europe that gave the totalitarian state, composed of one single party, such a good opportunity of taking the place of the constitutional liberal parliamentary state. For the totalitarian state, composed of one single party, is a European, and not solely a German phenomenon.

A great deal could be written about the various causes of the decline of liberal ideas in social and political affairs. I can give only a few brief hints:

(1) First, the *changes in social and economic structure* which took place in the nineteenth and twentieth centuries must be borne in mind. Modern industrial society, a mass society of innumerable individuals united by common needs, has taken the place of the former *bourgeois* society, consisting of a layer of economically independent notables who were the great landowners and *bourgeois*.

The First World War accelerated and intensified the process of economic and social levelling, by removing differences during wartime, especially in Germany. The whole of society was ground down into a uniform mass, grey as the soldiers; it was subjected to overall state control, to a totalitarian power which deeply affected even private life. It restricted the free expression of opinion, imposed censorship on the press, cut it off from all communication with foreign countries, and made it entirely dependent on the official information office, which accustomed the people to official communiqués which only very rarely divulged the whole truth, and in many cases suppressed, mutilated, or falsified it. More or less compulsory state or war loans swallowed up private incomes, later annihilated by inflation, which practically led to ruin and the end of fiduciary currency. Those possessing real estate (*Sachwertbesitzer*) had a monopoly, all the educated middle classes were impoverished, and large sections of society became solely dependent on state salaries and pensions or on private business; innumerable people who had been independent were so no longer.

As a result of such general changes, the party system on which the liberal state was founded was modified. Under the influence of universal suffrage, the parties were no longer composed of groups of notables, of clubs whose members were men who were socially and financially independent, who knew something about politics and were interested in them. They became mass organisations, directed by the electoral machine formed by a more or less highly organised party bureaucracy. The political agent took the place of the political idealist, and planned propaganda took the place of personal conviction and persuasion.

At the same time, the style and content of publications were changed. Political education, real discussion, individual thought ceased to be important; instead, what was required was mass appeal. In order to interest the masses, they must be attracted by sensationalism. He who is best at sensationalism is also the most popular. The most effective method is always the sermon of hatred, the least effective the voice of peaceable reason, since it makes the reader think, and even requires a certain wish to learn, and some knowledge.

(2) Similarly, *political intentions* changed. In the nineteenth century the struggle (particularly in Central Europe) was for national unity and for liberty guaranteed by a constitution — that is to say, for the participation of the governed in state affairs, for an assured, liberal legal system, and for protection against arbitrary acts. These were ideal ends, which had sprung mostly from spiritual impulses. By the end of the century they had been achieved in Italy and in Germany (with two exceptions).

In their place the economic preoccupations of modern industrial society came to the fore. The struggle for a higher standard of living became the main cause of internal

political differences; the idea of liberty was eclipsed by the idea of "social justice"; Liberalism was attacked and discarded in favour of Socialism. Political thought became more and more materialistic. Instead of being preoccupied by unity and liberty, it was interested in class conflicts, material interests, and the struggle for daily bread; in foreign policy the questions of the hour were *Lebensraum*, the great outlets and sources of raw materials, trading profits, and the rate of exchange.

So in general, politics stopped striving towards an ideal, and the prestige of parliaments declined. Since it had now become a matter of the interests of groups of people, the personal integrity of the representatives of these people is doubted. The details of their debates on economic subjects become more abstruse and uninteresting; the great complexity of modern economy partly controlled by the state, and the large number of opposing interests represented in parliament, make definite solutions, understood and approved by all, extremely rare. Therefore there is a great deal of discontent, and discontent breeds the summoning of a "strong man." The great groups of interests take "direct," extra-parliamentary action; there are strikes, the big workers' and employers' unions exert pressure on public opinion, there are processions, demonstrations, and mass meetings. The place of real debates is taken by announcements. Political struggles become more violent — he who has armed or semi-military partisans, ready to strike, at his call has the best chance of success.

Here, too, the World War accelerated and exaggerated this evolution. Like all great wars, it left behind it many adventurous spirits who were unable to settle down again to a *bourgeois* existence. They were nationalists, ready to serve any political adventurer who could use them for his "patriotic" activities. In *Mein Kampf* Hitler severely criticised the indiscipline of these eternal soldiers, without political aims, grouped together in bands (*Freikorps*), secret societies, and armed associations of all kinds, who sometimes supported and sometimes threatened republican governments. To him the fact that these armed bands and *Freikorps* had at times protected the republic from Communism showed nothing but unpardonable stupidity. He disapproved strongly of their Vehme murders, too, because they liquidated minor traitors without daring to deal with the "great November criminals."

In fact, however, many of these toughs became members of the *Sturmtruppen,* and the *Führerkorps* was mostly made up of them. There is a close connection between the SA and SS terrorists and these adventurous stragglers from the First World War. The inflation which took place in 1923, as a result of the war, left many people without money and with nothing to lose, so that they were ready to become political agents.

(3) *The changes in religious life* produced the same results. Christian teaching scarcely reached the populations of industrial towns; European civilisation became more and more secular as a result of the technical progress which took place in this rationalised and "unsupernatural" world. In Germany idealist philosophy, which had been a substitute for religion in *bourgeois* society for many years, began to be rejected, not in favour of philosophical materialism but of the modern "philosophy of life" which was spreading throughout Europe. This "philosophy of life" influenced large sections of society, and there was much talk of the supremacy of will, of biological explanations of mankind and of society, the glorification of physical strength, and of pure vitality, instead of a higher spirituality; the intellect and the rational were despised, while strong "instincts" (*Triebe*) and the vital impulse (the *élan vital* of H. Bergson) were admired. Nietzsche's doctrine of the superman and of the will to power as the prime force in the world, envisaged at first as an aristocratic ethical system, became in popular literature the deification of brutal mankind, of will to domination, of the eternal struggle for existence, of brute strength — though not without the complicity of that philosopher who unhesitatingly set the most daring aphorisms before the world. Darwinian ideas of the "survival of the fittest," of the eternal struggle for existence of all creatures, influenced all political thought. In all countries, including those of Western Europe, the age of imperialism brought with it books extolling the doctrine of might; with no knowledge of life, wars were no longer thought to be disasters for civilisation, but rather creative crises without which there could be no historical evolution.

Marxist theories were even more widespread, although not always recognised as such — the only political reality was the conflict of material interests, and political ideals were only ideological camouflage. (That this was a serious mistake is proved by all history, including that of National-Socialism.)

The example of the romanticism of the younger generation at the beginning of the twentieth century, with its scorn of *bourgeois* security and of reason and its call for "a dangerous life" and for exciting experience (*Erlebnis*), might lead one to believe that European countries were tired of the long period of peacefulness which had brought them their material well-being. Well-being and security were both destroyed by the First World War, which reduced society to a uniformity which could be touched only by mass violence and brutality.

This complete change of the political climate gave a new and troubling reality to the theories of Wilfredo Pareto about the eternal circular movement of activist *élites,* about the deceit of middle-class morality, and about the propelling force of deep feeling. The same was true of Georges Sorel's theories about "violence" and the "myth" which moves the masses, without the truth of its content having any importance. During their first phase, French syndicalists wished to replace old-style parliamentary groups by the ideal leader's party and militant *élite* which would pursue the aims of combat rather than the ideals of the *bourgeois* middle classes, and thus showed the young Mussolini his first and most pressing plan of action. The large-scale destruction of the war showed the way for futurist policies (in the meaning given to them by men like Gentile, Papini, and Marinetti) which refuse all connection with the authorities of the past.

(4) *New technical facilities for political propaganda* made the mobilisation of the masses much easier than it had been in the age of *bourgeoisies;* facilities such as loud-speakers, radio, a daily press rapidly printed in thousands of copies, lorries and motor-coaches which made possible the speedy deployment of political shock troops, almost limitless mass transport by railway, road, and air, so that it was possible to go proselytising from one end of the country to the other and to address a different mammoth meeting each evening. In 1922 40,000 Blackshirts formed ranks for the march on Rome, and caused a political panic simply on account of their numbers. At each of his national party congresses Hitler assembled and addressed some half a million men.

Thus did it become possible to make a reality of the theory of the sovereignty of the people, in a radical manner that was completely new. The masses could now be activated directly to become the political sovereign, and the roundabout method of the election of people's representatives to Parliament was no longer the only one.

It is clear that from the start the direct control of the "will of the people" was fundamental to democratic radicalism, unlike the Anglo-Saxon liberalism. The latter was originally founded not on the political rights of the many, but on the political privileges possessed by the various estates under feudalism, and which were perpetuated in the party groupings in modern parliaments. Groups of important people "represented" the people; in England these groups slowly became parties of the many during the nineteenth century.

The principle of direct sovereignty of the people, on the other hand, was in existence in the primitive democracy of the free American states in the seventeenth and eighteenth centuries. It was manifest in the town meetings of the settlers which constituted the first germs of American democracy; this principle is still in existence today, as shown by the President's position as a man on whom the nation, on whom every voter, but not Congress, can rely; before Congress his position is that of the executor of the will of the people.

Political compromise reached by discussion, the just balancing of the opposing desires and interests of different classes, groups, and individuals, belongs to the liberal parliamentary system. The nation is not regarded as a uniform mass of men, but as a collection of different individuals. The individual is important not only as a comrade of the people (*Volksgenosse*), but also as a person with claims on life and independent action.

Democratic radicalism, on the other hand, with terrible consistency, requires definite decisions instead of compromise. Sovereignty means deciding and not compromising. The best example of this rational principle is the idea, invented by Jean-Jacques Rousseau, of the "general will," an absolute idea which does not recognise any minority rights; if one opposes the general will it is because one has mistaken the general good (*Social Contract,* Book IV, chapter 2). The general will is the sworn enemy of individual intellect, of groups of individuals, because such groups are unaware of, or opposed to, the real public good; the more the individual intellect is overcome, the more probable it is that the real general will, the true interests of the people, will operate (*Social Contract,* Book II, chapter 3). Direct sovereignty of the people is infinitely preferable to any form of parliamentary government, for parliaments are the legacy of feudalism, and therefore the place in which private interests, and not the public good, struggle for supremacy (*Social Contract,* Book III, chapter 15).

Jean-Jacques Rousseau's general will became a myth at the time of the great revolution; aided by groups of individuals, it dominated parliamentary discussion and became increasingly intolerant. The people, now sovereign, is united in a popular political community (this was the most important innovation), a community of which each individual is part, although his particular rights are not protected (as Rousseau required). No appeal to higher authority is possible, because the people is sovereign, and there can be no appeal to ancient rights or privileges of the kind that was possible under the monarchy. Any one who opposes the will of the people is considered dangerously selfish, and therefore excludes himself from the community (this exclusion may then be made certain by banishment, imprisonment, or the guillotine).

How can the absolute and indivisible will of the people best be expressed? The best and simplest way, as Rousseau saw it, was the convocation of the sovereign people to a citizens' meeting, as in the classical city-state, the Swiss canton, or the American town meeting. But this form of direct democracy is of necessity limited to a very small community.

In large states there is the plebiscite which may be employed to show support for, and to be complementary to, the legislative machinery of parliament; for especially important laws, administrative decisions, and questions of foreign policy there would be a referendum. This system is cumbersome, costly, and difficult to operate, however, and does not really make possible a radical popular government.

A third method may be employed in large countries, however. The will of the people may be transferred to one man in whom confidence is reposed, who thus becomes an embodiment of the people, tangible and visible to all. Such a transference is made directly by the votes of the people, without passing through Parliament. . . .

The success of the twentieth-century dictatorships is conceivable only against this broad canvas of history. Of course they should not be considered in any way as the belated result of the French Revolution, or as having been influenced in any way by the works of Jean-Jacques Rousseau — this would be a very false interpretation of these historical remarks. Each of these dictatorships found its opportunity and its particular modern form in an extremely recent past.

Yet the latent possibility of a sudden change from radical democratic liberty to totalitarian tyranny is not modern. It grows where the great, socially disorganised, intellectually uniform masses in the modern city awaken to political consciousness, and where the former public authorities with their roots in the dim past (monarchy or parliamentary government) are destroyed or discredited. In such circumstances success seems assured if the distrust of a system of domination, already smouldering, is inflamed and a compact front is formed with a solid following. The masses are more ready to trust a living man than an anonymous institution.

Should a leader appear who is able to pass himself off as the representative of the most pure will of the people and as a real leader, then he will gain the support of the people, especially if he has a good few hard-hitting adherents. . . .

It is a very great mistake to believe that the modern function of leader of the people is in any way the heritage and continuation of the old, monarchic power of the princes. Neither Frederick the Great, Bismarck, nor Wilhelm II were the historical precursors of Adolf Hitler. His precursors were the demagogues and Caesars of modern history, from Danton to Lenin and Mussolini. It is also erroneous to see in the fanatical enthusiasm which millions of men felt for Hitler between 1930 and 1933 a continuation of the traditional veneration of Germans for their ancient princely houses. Our people's old attachment to its dynasties was, where it existed, the result of a traditional feeling; it was primarily caused by respect for a very ancient custom.

Hitler's party was, on the contrary, composed of numerous uprooted individuals whose mentality was revolutionary, who all consciously desired a new order, and who were convinced that their *Führer* was superior to any earlier leader. The characteristic of the Hitlerian movement which most strongly attracted the masses was its modernity, the fact that it was contemporary (facts which were brought out by the very far-flung technical apparatus used to gain support for the Party). Hitler's obscure, popular origins added to this attraction, and seemed an assurance that he could have nothing in common with the hated right-wing reactionaries — the great Junker land-owners, the officer class, and the great capitalists — even if he was sometimes obliged by force of circumstances to co-operate with people like Ludendorff and Hugenberg. Ludendorff himself declared himself opposed to Junker and capitalist prejudice, and a public-spirited friend of the people. Hitler and his supporters always contended that the electoral alliance established between the National-Socialists, the Stahlhelm group, and Hugenberg's party — the Harzburg Front of 1931 — was nothing more than a tactical agreement, for Hitler detested "all reaction." And when he opened negotiations with the big industrialists once more, being short of money and desirous of rapid success, Otto Strasser and the Schwarze Front, the most convinced revolutionary elements in the Party, deserted the cause and started an open rebellion. Later he was to seize every opportunity of condemning the "selfishness" of the capitalist class and stating how much his policy favoured the workers.

In any case, he did not wish to be a conservative, either socially or politically; he wished to be a revolutionary. But what did this revolution imply? What was the difference between his dictatorship and that of other modern dictators? What was specifically German in it, what could be only explained by specifically German historical events?

If the situation is simplified somewhat, one can answer that *Volksführer* Hitler's mission in history was to accomplish that which the Emperor and his Government had been unable to accomplish in the First World War: to weld the nation into a closed, warlike community under the leadership of a really popular *Führer,* respected by all. . . .

Wilhelm II only once succeeded in getting near the heart of the nation as a whole, on 4th August 1914, when he said to the *Reichstag* assembled in the Berlin castle: "I know parties no more, I only know Germans." These words had a tremendous effect. The idea of a popular, unified political community struck the people with the same effect that the French had experienced at the festival of the Federation on 14th July 1790. Yet this was an isolated incident; the new-found community broke up in conflicts about the aims of the war and its methods, and the Emperor's rule failed so completely that the German monarchy received a death-blow.

The Germans experienced a bitter disappointment when not only was the war lost in spite of tremendous efforts, terrible economic privation, and millions of deaths, but also when the popular community broke up instead of becoming stronger. The Right, bellicose nationalists out for conquest, and the Socialist leaders, who were opposed to imperialism and desirous of peace, no longer saw eye to eye. They attacked one another so violently, supporters of "victorious peace" (*Siegfrieden*) and "peace by agreement" (*Verständigungsfrieden*) the "prolongers of war" (*Kriegsverlängerer*) and "defeatists," as they described each other, that the nation was split into two halves.

This bitter conflict was the decisive and perhaps fundamental occurrence which led to the rise of National-Socialism. In comparison with this, all other considerations seem to me to be of secondary importance. Hitler's party was brought to power primarily by his efforts to overcome the old and fatal conflict between the nationalist *bourgeois* parties of the right and the masses of the left, the working and lower middle classes. It was not called the

"German workers' National-Socialist Party" (*National-sozialistische deutsche Arbeiterpartei*) in vain. The name was a programme in itself. . . .

Lacking any kind of critical ability, the masses saw in Hitler a saviour and a prophet, as he described in a voice hoarse with passion the violent brutalities committed by the victorious Powers on a defenceless Germany, as he promised that the criminals of November 1918 would be punished ("Some tens of thousands," he wrote in *Mein Kampf,* "shall one day expiate this crime against the state"); as he poured ridicule on the bungling of the "Marxist fumblers," as he pilloried the internal corruption of the "system of Weimar," or invoked the satanism of Bolshevism, or the grotesque spectre of an international conspiracy of Jews. No one asked how much this deluge of accusations contained of truth, exaggeration or slander, of wild invention or of lies. We can still remember the horror with which we saw this preaching of boundless hatred echoed in the newspapers of the period, and its effect on a public opinion which was both worried and contaminated.

It is extraordinary that these speeches filled with hatred were interpreted as the preparation for a new and more fundamental popular community (*Volksgemeinschaft*). Yet they were interpreted in this way. Many people were aware of the eccentric side of Hitler's visions of the future and of the fanaticism and furious passion of his movement. His *confrères,* shadows of demagogy, partly corrupt, partly suspect, and partly plebeian, were much more strongly criticised. It was realised that the minor leaders of the new movement were the men who had created disturbances at public meetings, and were therefore not worthy of confidence; the National-Socialist press was unreliable, its intellectual level very low, and its writings peculiar and of miserable quality. Nevertheless, the new popular community, the political and moral regeneration of the whole nation which was extolled in it, was regarded as an imposing doctrine, full of possibilities for the future.

How was such blindness possible? Was it the result of general decadence, of the disappearance of the tenets of religious morality? Did the German people lack moral instinct, and were they therefore unable to sense when a thing came from below? This lack of political and moral flair seems to be the most serious guilt with which the Germans who supported Hitler in these years can be reproached, and this reproach is not diminished by the fact that Germany was certainly not the only country to lack political and moral instinct where Hitler was concerned.

However, three factors must be taken into consideration. In the first place, calumnies, insults, and the moral abasement of the opposition are part of the normal equipment of every political struggle, and the violence with which this deplorable method is used varies only in degree. He who preaches distrust in a tottering government will always have great success in a modern mass democracy (as we have already remarked). And in Germany the political discussion was developing into a latent civil war; in a civil war strong fists are superior to all speeches and convictions. Of course, the peaceable *bourgeois* is inferior in such a sort of combat.

Secondly, it needed a high degree of moral and intellectual superiority to rest quiet and patient in such a situation as the Germans experienced in 1931–32, in the face of steadily growing millions of unemployed and of continual failures of foreign policy.

Thirdly, and more important, Hitler's demagogy was not restricted to negation alone. It gave the masses an admittedly indefinite conception of the future, but one which impressed them and aroused their enthusiasm. Hitler's criticism of existing Powers was not designed to cause despair, but to prepare the way for what he named the regeneration of the state and the people. The "chains of Versailles," he said, will be cast off as soon as Germany is regenerated from within, as soon as the will of the people really becomes assured, and thus permits a strong and definite leadership. The German people must put an end to the reign of numerous parties, must seize power from the November criminals, and place it in the hands of a national leadership; then Germany will be so great that the victorious Powers of Versailles will be obliged to give her her "right to life" (*Lebensrecht*) without a struggle. Germany must be strong, so as to be indispensable to other countries; then she will not lack allies.

First of all, Germany must be set in order. A definite plan of action in the field of economics was hardly mentioned. But Hitler's hearers, dazzled by the vision of a new and more glorious Germany, scarcely noticed this omission. The appeal to instincts of hatred was covered up by declarations of idealist and patriotic sentiments — virile courage, discipline, selfless readiness to serve the community, the tendency of all forces towards one great end: spontaneous devotion to the whole, the social brotherhood of all classes.

As in Mussolini's Italy, the ideal of brotherhood at the front, where in the World War there were no party or class differences, was extremely important. Hitler also adopted the ideal of military leadership and discipline as the best means of creating an orderly state. For the people, however, to be led was to co-operate voluntarily and not to be commanded; his followers (*Gefolgschaft*) were governed by fidelity to the *Führer*, himself an official carrying out the will of the people, who undertook on his side to be faithful to his followers.

Thus was born the false image of a moral community, which concealed the future dictator's lust for power. He was able to appeal simultaneously to the highest and lowest instincts. This mixture is always the most effective in politics — good and evil, noble and vile, truth, lies, and half-truths. . . .

SECURITY FOR A SICK PSYCHE?

Zevedei Barbu, the author of the first reading in this section, believes that the conditions which produce a dictatorship are very different from those which produce democracy. He believes that the disciplines of history, economics, and sociology must call upon help from his own field, social psychology, for explanations of phenomena such as Nazism. Barbu is the author of several studies in social psychology. Born in Rumania, he has been a diplomat as well as a scholar. He is now a lecturer in social psychology at the University of Glasgow in Scotland. Barbu emphasizes the uniqueness of German "national character," at least in the specific period 1918–1945. In the second reading, a prominent American anthropologist, Robert H. Lowie, cautions against any facile treatment of German "national character." Lowie, a professor at the University of California, is the author of a number of studies in the field of cultural anthropology.

The Uniqueness of the German Psyche, 1918-1933

ZEVEDEI BARBU

THE ANSWERS offered by the representatives of the economistic and sociologistic way of thought to the problem of the rise of Nazism, though illuminating in themselves, always leave the impression that something important has been omitted; that beyond class interest and ideological trends there lies a reality which, if known, offers a clue to this problem. We define this reality as a general state of mind characteristic of the German group as a whole during the inter-war period. Nazism is primarily an articulation at the political and cultural level of this state of mind. Nationalistic and socialistic trends of thought, controlled economy, as well as excess of militarism, are important features in the social climate leading to Nazism. But they are, rather, symptoms of a deeper reality of a psychological nature. A collective state of mind contains the factors which can explain both the tremendous success and the specific structure of Hitler's movement. Something more will be said, at a later stage, about the application of the concept of a collective state of mind in the present context. For the moment let us proceed to its description. Space only allows for a picture painted with a broad brush.

During the period of the rise of Nazism the German nation lived in unique conditions of stress and insecurity. The defeat of 1918 is usually mentioned as the starting point in the development of this situation. Quick structural changes such as the downfall of the monarchy, the collapse of the army, the appearance of new political parties are also important contributing factors. A series of inner contradictions and tensions within German society in the post-

From Zevedei Barbu, *Democracy and Dictatorship: Their Psychology and Patterns of Life* (New York, 1956), pp. 124–126, 128–130, and 156–157. Reprinted by permission of the Grove Press.

war period are in our opinion more important than the defeat itself, or the downfall of the Empire, for the understanding of this specific condition of stress and insecurity. Many demobilized soldiers and dismissed officers refused to go home and integrate themselves with the new conditions of life. They formed special military organizations, *Freikorps,* offering their protection to peasants threatened by raids of starving townsfolk, and to landlords from the eastern territories. And though the early Weimar régime used them in its struggle against the Communists, they became a menace to authority and security in the state by their independence and mercenary spirit. But, apart from the activities of the *Freikorps,* there were many other sources of instability and insecurity in the Weimar Republic. The Social Democrats were confused. Their manoeuvres between a strong Communist movement, deeply rooted in the German working classes, and the anti-Communist feelings of other classes and of the army in particular, resulted in a complete lack of orientation and of a programme. In this way, an inefficient government increased even more the frustration of the population. To this should be added a series of revolutionary attempts and Communist uprisings. Thus, the whole social atmosphere was loaded with tension, anxiety, and a spirit of brutality. The political parties took on a military character, each of them possessing fighting organizations.

The frustrating effects of economic crises, of unemployment, and particularly of the inflations of 1924 and 1929 are so well known that there is no need to enter into details. A word should be said about the contribution of the international scene to the situation of stress of the German group. Loss of colonies and national territories, military occupation, the reparation payments, and finally the French military occupation of the Ruhr district all intensified the insecurity. To all of this should be added the tensions caused in Bavaria — the birthplace of Nazism — by a series of separatist movements.

What are the most important psychological effects of this exceptional situation of stress? Perhaps the loss of the frame of reference for the behaviour of both group and individual is the most comprehensive symptom of this. The collapse of old institutions followed by a relatively long period of instability weakened and destroyed in many individuals the sense of discrimination and orientation in social life in particular. Since nothing remained unshaken, and certainly nothing unshakable, people swung from a state of naïvete to one of desperate incredulity. All opinions were equally good, or all equally meaningless. They lived in a *Meinungschaos* which produced in them apathy and complete detachment, and at the same time anxiety and readiness to do something, to do anything.

This state of mind affected, consciously or unconsciously, most individual members of German society. But the main problem for the social psychologist as well as for the political scientist is not the extension of this state of mind, but rather why a movement of the right, Hitler's movement, presented itself as the best answer to it. Why could not Socialism or Communism play this rôle, for both exploited the feelings of frustration and insecurity in the masses, and both promised a stable social order? The answer to these questions is, in essence, simple. The Nazis offered to the people the quickest and the most radical way of relief from a situation of stress and insecurity. While the Socialists kept on talking vaguely in the name of peace and democracy, while the Communists promised a narrow class policy, the Nazis attacked the Versailles Treaty, promised economic autarky and employment. While the Socialists tied up the destiny of Germany with that of European democracy, and the Communists with that of Soviet Russia, the Nazis stirred up the feeling of pride of a heroic nation which is not only the master of its own destiny, but is called upon to master the world.

In principle there could be no competition with this kind of language addressed to a group in a condition of stress. It gave immediate outlets for the feeling of guilt and for the need of aggression, and provided a solution to the need for security in the near future. The Socialists and Communists were doomed to failure since the Nazis provided for the deeper and more immediate needs of the masses. They spoke about dignity to the humiliated, about power to the defeated, about the organic stability of human society to people who were experiencing the ruin and disintegration of age-old institutions. The society they spoke of was not an idea, and not of the future, as was that propounded by the Communists, but of the past, of the glorious German past. . . .

THE SOCIAL COMPOSITION OF THE PARTY

It would be true to say that, sociologically, Nazism, as a political and spiritual movement, represents a cross-section of the German nation during the inter-war period. It answered a state of frustration and insecurity widespread in all strata of the population during this period. It would also be right to infer from this that the cadres, and particularly the leadership of the party, were made up of individuals and groups who suffered more than others from frustration and insecurity.

The core of the party was formed by socially nondescript people, frustrated in their efforts to achieve a certain status in their society, the prototype of whom is Hitler. The demobilized soldiers and officers, former members of the *Freikorps,* formed an important Nazi group. Goering and Röhm are typical. Unemployed youngsters, émigrés, and students also found a point of attraction in the movement. To this is added a number of intellectuals frustrated in their aspirations, as Goebbels was, or incapable of adjusting themselves to the cultural climate of their time and consequently escaping into the mythical world of the past, like those belonging to the Thule Society of Munich. From the historically constituted classes Nazism attracted in the first place the peripheral elements. From the working class it attracted "the flotsam, the strugglers living on the fringe of their own class, the workers of odd jobs, and the unemployed." In the upper classes the party appealed in particular to aristocrats who identified themselves with a highly inadequate concept of their own class; they joined the party in order to re-make the position once held by the Junkers in Imperial Germany. Peasants who were by their aspirations above their group, or by their poverty below it, were also attracted to the movement.

All the individuals and groups mentioned above have one trait in common: they all can be called *déclassés,* that is, people who failed completely or partly to integrate themselves with one of the institutionalized forms of their society. They also suffer from lack of social attachment. In this way the *déclassés* can, by analogy with psychopathic personality, be described as sociopathic personalities. As the psychopathics are liable to all forms of delinquency, so are the sociopathics liable to political delinquency in particular, that is, they are breakers of the political order of their own society. More will be said later about the connexion between psychopathic and sociopathic personality. For the moment we consider the sociopathic personality in itself. It should be mentioned in the first place that industrial society has a great capacity for creating sociopathic groups. Its fluid character and its rapid growth are among the main causes of this phenomenon. The impersonal character of this society and the mechanical type of integration required by it have also contributed to this. The situation of post-war Germany is characteristic from this point of view. The instability of that period forms an additional factor contributing to the creation of non-integrated individuals and groups.

The Nazi movement can be considered as the meeting point of all individuals and groups with an unstable social status; it evolved as a result of the disrupting processes taking place in the post-war period. It is, therefore, the classless element, rather than a particular social class, that should first be considered in order to understand Nazism. As opposed to any socialist party — obviously a class party — and to any democratic party normally based on a particular social group, Nazism represents in its structure the entire nation on a reduced scale. This is one of the first factors determining its totalitarian character.

STATE OF MIND, OR NATIONAL CHARACTER

Few psychologists interested in the origins of Nazism could escape the temptation of using the concept of national character. Most of them deal at large with the "famous" and "perennial" Germanic aggression, with the Germanic mysticism, ethnocentrism, authoritarian family, etc. Though far from expressing a definite opinion on this point, we feel that the concept of the national character is too much of a theoretical construct. Examples of aggression, collective or individual, can easily be found in every nation. Consequently we started to trace the origins of Nazism in a collective state of mind historically limited to the inter-war period. This is the state of mind created in a group of individuals under conditions of stress. A rigid social organization, certain mystical inclinations, group-centrism and aggression are normally involved in the behaviour of a group living under such conditions. To us the problem of the German national character is secondary as a determining factor in the rise of Nazism. . . .

SOCIOGENESIS

Can one explain the origins of the pathological aspects of Nazism only by the presence of certain psychopathological traits in the Nazi leaders, or has one to resort, for the solution of this problem, to certain qualities of contemporary German society and culture? One is on safe ground when talking about the presence of psychopathological traits in Hitler and other Nazi leaders from the simple fact that a certain amount of empirical evidence is available. In his study, Gilbert made use of reliable psychological methods. But when trying to analyse

the pathological elements involved in the German culture-pattern, during the period preceding Nazism, one can hardly rely on any systematic research, psychological or anthropological. In this case the psychologist's only choice is to give his own interpretation to a series of historical facts selected by him as symptomatic for the mental structure of the German group during the period under consideration. The hypothetical elements have to be very strong indeed. And yet, this hypothesis seems to be necessary. For Hitler's paranoia or Goering's narcissistic traits, symptomatic as they were, could hardly create a series of psychopathological trends in the Nazi group, or in the German group, had they met indifferent or hostile surroundings. The fact is that they built themselves on elements found already in German society and culture.

In what follows we describe some of the main aspects of contemporary German society and culture which disclose the existence of certain abnormal and pathological traits in the individuals belonging to this society and culture.

1. The concept most accurately covering the main pathological symptoms shown by German society during and immediately preceding Nazism is that of a sociopathic group. As in the case of sociopathic personality, the sociopathic character of the group is motivated by a basic insecurity, and, as in the case of psychopathic personality again, the acting out of the feeling of insecurity leads to a morbid urge for self-assertion of the group. Hence the authoritarian character of its organization, its policy based on force, and its anti-social behaviour.

Insecurity can be considered as the main cause of German society's failure to adjust itself to twentieth-century democratic civilization; it prevented the German group from projecting its aspirations on the values created by this civilization. This basic insecurity destroyed the frame of reference for the aspirations of the German group.

The lack of an adequate frame of reference has a particular sociological importance, which in the case of Nazism has received too little attention. This is the group trait that can explain to a great extent the importance played by the *déclassés* and psychopathic personalities of the Nazi movement. For it is this sociological category and this personality type that can more successfully crystallize the various mental factors in a group with a lost frame of reference. Its disorientation, its fears and revolt against a hostile environment, and finally its urge to escape into adventure,

all these find their highest expression in that type of personality and group described by us as sociopathic.

We hasten to say that we cannot describe the whole of the twentieth [century] German society as having a well-defined sociopathic structure. Its general state of insecurity and its incapacity to integrate with European democratic civilization can be considered only as a fertile ground in which a sociopathic structure could develop. . . .

Germans Are Like Other Europeans

ROBERT H. LOWIE

THE QUESTION of how Germans reacted to the anti-Jewish program of the National Socialist party merges into the wider problem of how they reacted to the Nazi program in its totality and how they reacted and are likely to react to the democratic principles which the Western Allies regard as essential for international safety.

The first thing to note is that relevant attitudes of Germans were not stationary during the years of Nazi rise and ascendancy; indeed, the chronological factor is all-important. Let us then try to picture an average German confronted with the situation between 1918 and 1933. The disastrous first World War had brought spiritual and material distress. Patriots writhed under the stipulations of the peace treaty, which assailed Germany as the sole nation guilty of starting the war, deprived her of her colonies, reduced her European territory, and imposed heavy reparations. The victors flouted the new republican government, making it constantly lose face before

its own people, to many of whom the concept of a free commonwealth was strange and repulsive. In consequence, the Weimar regime weakened until at times it ceased to govern large sections at all. It was unable to enforce federal legislation in Bavaria. It was unable to prevent the assassination of its officials. It was unable to thwart the murderous brawls of contending factions. The boasted order that had reigned in the empire was irretrievably gone. Economically, an unprecedented inflation wiped out fortunes and beggared all whose income was derived from pensions or fixed salaries. In the fall of 1923 Driesch paid 16 billion marks for a streetcar ticket; in 1924 I paid a million and a quarter crowns a week at my boarding-house in Vienna and tipped the maid a hundred and fifty thousand. Stabilization of the monetary unit did, indeed, bring relief, but only temporarily; and when the world crisis reached the Reich, it brought havoc once more in its wake. One chancellor after another tried to do away with unemployment and high

From Robert H. Lowie, *Toward Understanding Germany* (Chicago, 1954), pp. 328–331 and 354–356. Reprinted by permission of the University of Chicago Press.

prices, but failed. In 1929 the number of jobless Germans was 2,895,000; at the end of 1930 the figure had risen to 3,250,000. Hitler made extravagant promises, but the people were in a mood to catch at any straw that might lift them from their Slough of Despond. Even so, it should not be forgotten that in November, 1932, only 33.1 per cent of the voters supported Hitler, and even in the last "free" election under his regime he had won over only 43.9 per cent.

It may be asked, nevertheless, why so large a minority could possibly lend ear to an uneducated rabble-rouser whose book had flaunted the most extreme and in part repulsive doctrines. Germans answer that though many bought *Mein Kampf*, few read it or much of it; and those who did assumed, plausibly enough, that its most radical utterances were never meant to be followed up by action. Again, those who perused the allegedly immutable program of the party found little there to recoil from on moderately liberal principles, apart from the racialist paragraphs, and even these were not couched in offensive language. The platform opposed the spoils system. It demanded a greater Germany, but the Allies themselves had proclaimed the principle of self-determination and of the national state, though they had repudiated it as regards Austria. The platform postulated the state's duty "to promote the industry and livelihood of citizens," all of whom were to enjoy equal rights and obligations. War profiteering was to be squashed by ruthless confiscation. There was promise of ampler old age pensions and of a far-reaching land reform. Gifted children of poor parents were to be educated at the expense of the state, which was further pledged to raise the standard of health by banning child labor and by furthering physical training. To be sure, the program also contained ominous suggestions of a controlled press; and, of course, we now know that the subsequent masters of Germany's destiny were really interested, above all, in gaining and preserving des-

potic control of the country. But the impoverished, jobless, politically naïve man in the street, longing for delivery from present evils, did not know it. He was neither a skeptical analyst nor a prophet: he wanted precisely one thing — relief from an unbearable present.

It is important to note that this relief, whatever its means, actually came. A Swiss colleague who attended the University of Berlin in 1933 told me that he was struck by the rapidity of a change for the better. The dismal sight of woebegone men and women begging for alms suddenly vanished completely. As a former Nazi states: "People were once more laughing and singing in Germany; they were hoping and had once more a sense of secure existence. The meanest laborer knew that he would never again be jobless, never without provision and help."

The same writer, who remarks that young people conceived the new movement as directly the reverse of what Hitler made of it, goes on to say: "What convinced us at the time of National Socialism was the fact that it made new, better men out of people we knew. There was the lazy-bones who suddenly sacrificed his leisure time and holidays without receiving compensation. There was the beaten-up, hospitalized SA who in his delirium yearned for his next performance of duty; there were miserly peasants who furnished potatoes, fat, and hams for the SA auxiliary kitchens. There were the youngsters who, with radiant eyes, rendered a thousand services and often were in despair because they were not yet old enough to 'march' along with us." Similarly, the historian Meinecke, who was not a Nazi, declares that National Socialism had an immense number of harmless, uncritical, decent, and even idealistic fellow-travelers.

For men of all classes outside the ranks of intransigent cosmopolitans, the sudden rise of Germany in the international theater was a matter of the utmost moment. The Allies had harassed and intimidated the republican government, had insisted on the admission of German guilt, to the humiliation of all German patriots, including the majority of Social Democrats. But when Hitler began to talk, the Allies changed their tune; the bullies of the 1920's turned into the cravens of the 1930's. According to Pechel, a sufferer from Nazi vengeance, nothing gave the resistance movement a greater setback than the concessions now made to the dictator when they had been denied to a moderate republican government. The contention is plausible, for apparently no national group is immune to the charm of power when wielded by its own head. The English glory in the days of Elizabeth I and Cromwell, considering the atrocities of their reigns little more than venial peccadilloes; and Napoleon still lies in state in the Invalides. Hence the gain Hitler secured for his country in point of international prestige inevitably won over the hearts of innumerable compatriots at the beginning of his leadership. Later, when the true nature of his designs had become clear, effective open counteraction was no longer possible. On this subject our ex-Nazi 693044 says: "Since 1945 people have more than amply preached to us that even before the war we ought to have chased Hitler to the devil. We ought to have seen that he was fomenting war, that he was planning crimes. This chasing to the devil is a thoroughly excellent idea, only no one has revealed the recipe how that is to be done in an authoritarian state." The same man reveals the mentality of his type in further confessions: "If now someone were to ask me, 'Do you repent for having been a National Socialist?' I must answer, 'No! I repent that my faith was misused on behalf of an evil cause, I repent every unexpiable crime committed in my and my comrades' name, I repent that the faith and unheard-of self-sacrifice and devotion of German workers was betrayed by Hitler — but I do not repent having loved my people above everything, that I rendered every sacrifice, that I believed and

hoped.' In a French author I read a formula that consoled me: 'It is finer and better ardently to serve a great error than pettily to drudge for a petty truth.'"

The motives that drove the masses into the Nazi ranks have been dispassionately summarized along similar lines by a strong anti-Nazi of the old conservative type. It was the promise of work and bread, the feeling of solidarity the people at large were yearning for, Silens contends, that proved the great drawing card. Germans were *not* craving a world war, had no desire to conquer the world, to persecute and exterminate human groups. They acclaimed Hitler for apparently assuring peace and employment, not as the leader of an offensive war, of clandestine crimes and atrocities. Many initially regarded the ranting against Jews as mere campaign claptrap. Very few party members read Rosenberg's *Mythos des 20. Jahrhunderts*, the official exposition of the Nazi world view. Silens even conjectures that though millions bought *Mein Kampf*, few read it through; and educated readers did not take seriously what seemed incredible or nonsensical in it. . . .

We cannot repeat too often that no finding about the Germans is scientifically valid until we know the distribution of the phenomena in space and time. No trait, no attitude, is *the* German trait or attitude unless it is pan-German and pan-diachronically so; and it is not distinctively German unless it is found only among Germans. By this test, the Bavarian is farther from the Hamburger than the Hamburger from the Briton; the Viennese proletarian has more affinity with a Danish worker than with a Styrian peasant. There is not only regional and class differentiation among Germans, but the differences are such as to align some Germans with aliens rather than with fellow-Germans. The concept of a German culture sphere with which we have been tentatively operating thus turns out to be an ill-defined, if not indefinable, entity.

If anything, the differences within the same people at different periods is even more instructive — witness the history of national literatures. Elizabethan England was healthily unrestrained; the Puritans, in reaction, closed theaters, flogged actors, and put the press "under the guardianship of austere licensers"; Restoration authors, re-acting in turn, dropped all pretense to de-cency (Macaulay). It would be absurd to suppose that "the English" by mutation completely and repeatedly changed their innate character in three successive genera-tions. What happened was obviously that certain literary leaders impressed their indi-viduality on their contemporaries and that leaders of a different mentality succeeded in stamping *theirs* on the following genera-tion. Sane exuberance, priggish zealotry, and abandoned profligacy are human phe-nomena likely to be found everywhere; which of them becomes typical at a certain stage of a country's literature depends on historical circumstances.

In retrospect, it is from this point of view that the remarkable alterations in Ger-man orientation from 1750 until the pres-ent find partial explanation. Not all Eng-lishmen were priggish zealots under the Puritans, not all of them were reckless libertines under Charles II; both types co-existed throughout, each merely "going underground" when the other gained tem-porary ascendancy. In Germany there was corresponding alternation of polar trends: particularism and centralism became alter-nately dominant and recessive, as did cos-mopolitanism and nationalism. That either eliminated the other for good is an illusion.

Of course, not all the differences that have divided Germany from other Western countries can be regarded in this way. The effects of industrialism do not seem to be cyclic but rather appear as a sequence of irreversible phenomena. The fundamental fact here seems to be simply that Germany, becoming industrialized later than Eng-land, showed the social consequences of industrialism later, say as regards family life. Again, the comparative approach cor-rects first impressions. The status of Ger-man women, legally and practically, has not been inferior to that of Spanish, Italian, or French women. Further, it has altered with changing conditions, which have brought it more in line with Anglo-Saxon standards. Even the ideology of naziism was able to arrest the development only for a brief period before the second World War.

Germans, then, cannot easily be treated as a unit marked off from the rest of West-ern civilization. Their alleged patriarchal-ism, their love of military glory, their fond-ness for abstract principles, can all be paralleled in French culture. The political incompetence deplored by the Germans themselves can hardly be an immutable trait in the light of Alemannic history.

It is when particular social strata are set beside their equivalents elsewhere that convincing contrasts appear. The yearning for titles in the upper classes has certainly — with a partial exception in Switzerland and the Hanseatic cities — been obtrusive throughout the last two centuries. As pointed out, the failure to evolve the "gen-tleman" concept is enviously admitted by Germans themselves. With this lack may be correlated that intemperateness in con-troversy, that substitution of uninhibited violence for sober judgment, that "method-ical vehemence" (Röpke) which so fre-quently mars the utterances of educated Germans. Every nation has its scum, but one does not expect a Schopenhauer to revile a Hegel in the language of a gutter-snipe, nor the venomous obscenities of the Viennese students inspired by Schönerer. As Röpke says, his countrymen tend to ex-tremism, exaggerating bad as well as good ideas, carrying them out to their very last consequences.

Such intensity has its positive aspect in German thoroughness, whether in research or in the household, in the love for work as an end in itself. In one of its noblest forms it appears as the proletarian's craving for intellectual and aesthetic culture.

The contention, then, is not that Germans are exactly like other peoples, but rather that western Europe as a whole presents a continuum — one culture area with admittedly innumerable local variations. This impression is deepened when we take into account the demonstrable changes in dominant outlook during the last two centuries in every country involved. Again the history of national literatures furnishes a clue to understanding. French letters and formal restraint are commonly taken as synonymous, but France had her Rabelais and Victor Hugo as well as her Racine. Let us get away from stereotypes. When the cultures of Britain, France, Italy, and Spain are once studied from the comparative point of view, we shall have a sounder factual basis for dividing the western European area into cultural subdivisions than the inexpensive one of national or even linguistic boundaries.

SUGGESTIONS FOR ADDITIONAL READING

National Socialism should be studied against the broad background of European and German history. Useful recent surveys of German history have been published by Ralph Flenley, *Modern German History* (New York, 1953), and Koppel S. Pinson, *Modern Germany, Its History and Civilization* (New York, 1954). Another major survey of modern German history is presently nearing completion by Hajo Holborn. The sympathetic discussion of German "national character" by the American anthropologist Robert H. Lowie, *Toward Understanding Germany* (Chicago, 1954) may be appropriately read as a companion piece to the highly critical volume by Louis L. Snyder, *German Nationalism . . .* (Harrisburg, Pennsylvania, 1952). The standard history of the development of political parties in Germany is Ludwig Bergsträsser, *Geschichte der politischen Parteien in Deutschland*, 9th ed. (Munich, 1955). Students who wish to acquire detailed knowledge of the more immediate historical background of the Nazi revolution should study the Bismarckian Empire of 1870–1918, wartime and revolutionary Germany, 1914–1919, and the Weimar Republic of 1919–1933. Valuable volumes for this are: Adalbert Wahl (conservative), *Deutsche Geschichte von der Reichsgründung bis zum Ausbruch des Weltkrieges*, 4 vols. (Stuttgart, 1926–1936); Johannes Ziekursch (liberal), *Politische Geschichte des neuen deutschen Reiches*, 3 vols. (Cologne, 1925–1930); Edmond Vermeil, *L'Allemagne contemporaine: sociale, politique et culturelle, 1890–1950*, 2 vols. (Paris, 1952–1953); the exceedingly important documentary collection by Ralph Haswell Lutz (ed.), *Fall of the German Empire, 1914–1918*, 2 vols. (Stanford University, 1932); Arthur Rosenberg (socialist), *The Birth of the German Republic . . .* (London, 1931); the history by John L. Snell, *Germany Enters the Democratic Era*, which should appear in 1959; and S. W. Halperin, *Germany Tried Democracy . . .* (New York, 1946).

For the rise of Nazism, see first the volumes from which the readings in this booklet have been selected: Alan Bullock, *Hitler: A Study in Tyranny* (New York, 1952); Hans Kohn (ed.), *German History: Some New German Views* (Boston, 1954), for the essay by Ludwig Dehio and other important interpretations by Karl Buchheim, Hans Herzfeld, Alfred von Martin, Franz Schnabel, Hajo Holborn, Friedrich Meinecke, and others; another collection of essays, essential to any mature grasp of the causes and character of Nazism, by Maurice Baumont, John H. E. Fried, Edmond Vermeil and others, *The Third Reich* (New York, 1955), especially the chapters by Maurice Baumont, J. J. Schokking, Léon Poliakov, and Gerhard Ritter, from which readings in this booklet have been taken, and the essays by Alan Bullock, A. J. P. Taylor, Otto Klineberg, and Henry Pachter; the English condensation of the 2 vol. work mentioned above by Edmond Vermeil, *Germany in the Twentieth Century . . .* (New York, 1956), which is inadequate, but fairly presents Vermeil's views in essence and provides a reading in this booklet; A. J. P. Taylor, *The Course of German History: A Survey of the Development of Germany since 1815* (New York, 1946); essay by E. N. Anderson in G. A. Almond (ed.), *The Struggle for Democracy in Germany* (Chapel Hill, 1949); the vivid but far from definitive book by Milton Mayer, *They Thought They Were Free* (Chicago, 1955), for information on the role of anti-Semitism and fear of Communism in the rise of Nazism; Franz L. Neumann, *Behemoth: The Structure and Practice of National Socialism* (London, New York, and Toronto, 1942); George W. F. Hallgarten, "Adolf Hitler and German Heavy Industry, 1931–1933," *Journal of Economic History*, XII (Summer 1952), 222–246; Friedrich Meinecke, *The German Catastrophe* (Cambridge, Mass., 1950); Gerard Braunthal, "The German Free Trade Unions during the Rise of Nazism," *Journal of Central European Affairs*, XV (January, 1956), 339–353; Robert G. L. Waite, *Vanguard of Nazism: The Free Corps in Postwar Germany, 1918–1923* (Cambridge, Mass., 1952); Gordon A. Craig, *The Politics of the Prussian Army, 1640–1945* (Oxford, 1955); Gerhard Ritter, "The Military and Politics in Germany," *Journal of Central European Affairs*, XVII (October, 1957), 259–271; Zevedei Barbu, *Democracy and Dictatorship: Their Psychology and Patterns of Life* (New York, 1956); and Robert H. Lowie, *Toward Understanding Germany* (Chicago, 1954).

Works by various other authors whose views were reflected in the introduction to this booklet are useful and interesting. Those not already listed in this bibliography are as follows: Geoffrey Barraclough, "History, Morals, and Politics," *International Affairs*, XXXIV (January, 1958), 1–15; Karl Dietrich Bracher, *Die Auflösung der Weimarer Republic*, 2nd ed. (Stuttgart and Düsseldorf, 1957); T. L. Jarman, *The Rise and Fall of Nazi Germany* (New York, 1956); William M. McGovern, *From Luther to Hitler* . . . (Boston, New York, and Chicago, 1941); Jean Edouard Spenlé, *La Pensée allemande de Luther à Nietzsche*, 3rd ed. (Paris, 1942); Peter Viereck, *Metapolitics from the Romantics to Hitler* (New York, 1941); Friedrich Glum, *Philosophen im Spiegel und Zerrspiegel* . . . (Munich, 1954); Jean Neurohr, *Der Mythos vom Dritten Reich* . . . (Stuttgart, 1957); Fritz Richard Stern, *Cultural Despair and the Politics of Discontent* . . . (Ann Arbor, Mich., 1954), a microfilm copy of a Columbia University doctoral dissertation; Waldemar Gurian, *Um des Reiches Zukunft* . . . (Freiburg-im-Breisgau, 1932); Armin Mohler, *Die Konservative Revolution in Deutschland 1918–1932* (Stuttgart, 1950); Klemens von Klemperer, *Germany's New Conservatism* . . . (Princeton, 1957); Edmond Vermeil, *Doctrinaires de la Révolution Allemande (1918–1938)* (Paris, 1939); Kurt Sontheimer, "Antidemokratisches Denken in der Weimarer Republik," *Vierteljahrshefte für Zeitgeschichte*, V (January, 1957), 42–62; Hannah Arendt, *The Origins of Totalitarianism* (New York, 1951); Paul W. Massing, *Rehearsal for Destruction: A Study of Political Anti-Semitism in Imperial Germany* (New York, 1949); Ossip K. Flechtheim, *Die Kommunistische Partei Deutschlands in der Weimarer Republik* (Offenbach-am-Main, 1948); Ruth Fischer, *Stalin and German Communism* . . . (Cambridge, Mass., 1948); Lewis J. Edinger, *German Exile Politics* . . . (Berkeley, 1956); T. W. Adorno, Else Frenkel-Brunswik, D. J. Levinson, and R. N. Sanford, *The Authoritarian Personality* (New York, 1950); Edward A. Shils, "Authoritarianism: 'Right' and 'Left'," in the symposium by Richard Christie and Marie Jahoda (eds.), *Studies in the Scope and Method of "The Authoritarian Personality"* (Glencoe, Ill., 1954), pp. 24–49, and especially 32–33; Werner Liebe, *Die Deutschnationale Volkspartei 1918–1924* (Düsseldorf, 1956); Walter H. Kaufmann, *Monarchism in the Weimar Republic* (New York, 1952); Telford Taylor, *Sword and Swastika* (New York, 1952); John W. Wheeler-Bennett, *The Nemesis of Power: The German Army in Politics, 1918–1945* (New York, 1953); Harold J. Gordon, Jr., *The Reichswehr and the German Republic, 1919–1926* (Princeton, 1957); Gerhard Ritter, *Staatskunst und Kriegshandwerk* (Munich, 1954), the first volume of an impressive history of the role of the army in modern German history; Werner T. Angress, "The Peasants in the Revolution of 1918 and the Rise of Nazism," to appear soon in the *Journal of Central European Affairs*; Sigmund Neumann, *Die deutschen Parteien* . . . (Berlin, 1932), and, by the same author, *Permanent Revolution: The Total State* . . . (New York and London, 1942); Erich Fromm, *Escape from Freedom* (New York, 1941); William L. Langer,

"The Next Assignment," *American Historical Review*, LXIII (January, 1958), 283–304; and Andrew G. Whiteside, "The Nature and Origins of National Socialism," *Journal of Central European Affairs*, XVII (April, 1957), an exceptionally useful review of some twenty years of changing interpretations of Nazism.

Only a few of the many other books about various aspects of National Socialism can be listed here. Among those of most general interest are: Theodore Abel, *Why Hitler Came into Power* . . . (New York, 1938); Gabriel A. Almond (ed.), *The Struggle for Democracy in Germany* (Chapel Hill, 1949); Rohan Butler, *The Roots of National Socialism* (London, 1941); C. B. Hoover, *Germany Enters the Third Reich* (New York, 1933); Henri Lichtenberger, *The Third Reich*, trans. by Koppel S. Pinson (New York, 1937); Gerhard Ritter, *Europa und die deutsche Frage* . . . (Munich, 1947); Hermann Rauschning, *The Revolution of Nihilism* (New York, 1939); and Frederick L. Schumann, *The Nazi Dictatorship* (New York, 1936). See the biographies of Hitler by: Konrad Heiden, *Der Fuehrer: Hitler's Rise to Power* (Boston, 1944); August Kubizek, *The Young Hitler I Knew* (Boston, 1955); and Otto Dietrich, *12 Jahre mit Hitler* (Munich, 1955). Hitler's speeches have been collected by: Norman H. Baynes (ed.), *The Speeches of Adolf Hitler* . . . , 2 vols. (London, New York, and Toronto, 1942); Gordon W. Prange, *Hitler's Words* (Washington, 1944); and Raoul de Roussy de Sales (ed.), *My New Order* (New York, 1941). Scattered conversations by Hitler, often banal, often amazing, but always revealing, have been published in English translation by H. R. Trevor-Roper under the title *Hitler's Secret Conversations, 1941–1944* (New York, 1953). Hitler's propagandistic autobiography, *Mein Kampf*, is available in several editions in English and German; autobiographical volumes and other writings by many of the top Nazi leaders are available under their names in library card catalogues. On Nazi govern-

mental structure and domestic policies see: William Ebenstein, *The Nazi State* (New York and Toronto, 1943); Fritz Morstein Marx, *Government in the Third Reich* (New York and London, 1937); J. K. Pollock, *The Government of Greater Germany* (New York, 1938); Otto Nathan, *The Nazi Economic System* . . . (Durham, 1944); Maxine Sweezy, *The Structure of Nazi Economy* (Cambridge, Mass., 1941); Earl R. Beck, *Verdict on Schacht* . . . (Tallahassee, Florida, 1956); Edward Norman Peterson, *Hjalmar Schacht: For and Against Hitler* . . . (Boston, 1954); and, for the background of one feature of Nazi economics, Ralph Bowen, *German Theories of the Corporative State* (New York, 1947); also: Edward Y. Hartshorne, *The German Universities and National Socialism* (Cambridge, Mass., 1937); G. F. Kneller, *The Educational Philosophy of National Socialism* (New Haven, 1941); Arthur Frey, *Cross and Swastika: The Ordeal of the German Church* (London, 1938); Nathanial Micklem, *National Socialism and the Roman Catholic Church* (London, New York, and Toronto, 1939); Clifford Kirkpatrick, *Nazi Germany: Its Women and Family Life* (Indianapolis and New York, 1938); Hellmut Lehmann-Haupt, *Art Under a Dictatorship* (London, 1954); and Eugen Kogon, *The Theory and Practice of Hell* . . . (New York, 1941), which describes concentration camp policies and conditions.

Foreign policies are discussed by: Gordon A. Craig and Felix Gilbert (eds.), *The Diplomats, 1919–1939* (Princeton, 1953); John A. Lukacs, *The Great Powers and Eastern Europe* (New York, 1953); Paul Seabury, *The Wilhelmstrasse: A Study of German Diplomats under the Nazi Regime* (Berkeley, 1954); G. L. Weinberg, *Germany and the Soviet Union, 1939–41* (Leiden, 1954); John W. Wheeler-Bennett, *Munich: Prologue to Tragedy* (London, 1948). For Hitler's attempts to create a "New Order" in Europe, 1939–45, see Arnold Toynbee (ed.), *Hitler's Europe* (London, 1955) and Alexander Dallin,

German Rule in Russia, 1941–1945 (New York, 1957). On the anti-Nazi resistance movements within Germany see Gerhard Ritter, *Carl Goerdeler und die deutsche Widerstandsbewegung* (Stuttgart, 1955), which has been published in English as: *The German Resistance: Carl Goerdeler's Struggle against Tyranny* (New York, 1958); Hans Rothfels, *The German Opposition to Hitler* (Chicago, 1948); and the following works: Constantine Fitzgibbon, *20 July* (New York, 1956); Wilhelm von Schramm, *Conspiracy among Generals* (New York, 1956); and Mary A. Gallin, *Ethical and Religious Factors in the German Resistance to Hitler* (Washington, 1955). The end of the affair is told by Georges Blond, *The Death of Hitler's Germany* (New York, 1954), and H. R. Trevor-Roper, *The Last Days of Hitler* (New York, 1947).

Among the most important published documents are: *Documents on German Foreign Policy, 1918–1945*, series C and D, edited by Paul Sweet and others (Washington, 1949–); Ministry of Foreign Affairs of the U.S.S.R., *Documents and Materials Relating to the Eve of the Second World War*, 2 vols. (Moscow, 1948); and the various records of the Nuremberg tribunals, especially: *Nazi Conspiracy and Aggression*, 10 vols. (Washington, 1946–1948); *The Trial of German Major War Criminals*, 22 vols. (Washington, 1946–1950); and *The Trial of the Major War Criminals before the International Military Tribunal: Proceedings and Documents*, 42 vols. (Nuremberg, 1947–1949). See also: Johannes Hohlfeld (ed.), *Dokumente der Deutschen Politik und Geschichte von 1848 bis zur Gegenwart*, 8 + vols. (Berlin and Munich, 1951–).

Those who wish to do research in primary source materials on Nazism should also consult the excellent bibliography in Alan Bullock's biography of Hitler. The following more lengthy or more specialized bibliographies should then be consulted: Waldo Chamberlin, *Industrial Relations in Germany, 1914–1939: Annotated Bibliography of Materials in the Hoover Library . . .* (Stanford University, 1942), and Hildegard R. Boeninger, *The Hoover Library Collection on Germany* (Stanford University, 1955); the publications of the Wiener Library (London), especially its *Bulletin* and the following bibliographies: *From Weimar to Hitler: Germany, 1918–1933* (London, 1952); *Books on Persecution, Terror, and Resistance in Nazi Germany* (London, 1949), with *Supplement* (London, 1953); and *German Jewry: Its History, Life and Culture . . . to 1945* (London, 1958); Centre de Documentation Juivre Contemporaine (Paris), *Catalogue des Ouvrages Publiés par le Centre . . . 1945–1958* (Paris, 1958); Gerhard L. Weinberg, Fritz T. Epstein, and others, *Guide to Captured German Documents* (Maxwell Field, Ala., 1952); German and other doctoral dissertations, which are listed in Alfred Milatz and Thilo Vogelsang (eds.), *Hochschulschriften zur neueren deutschen Geschichte*, 1st ed.: *1945–1955* (Bonn, 1956); and the files of the *Journal of Modern History* (Chicago), *International Affairs* (London) and, most especially, the *Journal of Central European Affairs* (Boulder, Colorado) and the *Vierteljahrshefte für Zeitgeschichte* (Tübingen). See also the various *Guides to German Records Microfilmed at Alexandria, Va.*, issued by the National Archives, and especially No. 3: *Records of the National Socialist German Labor Party* (Washington, 1958). Copies of these *Guides* and microfilm copies of the Nazi records may be purchased from the National Archives.